The Walter Lynwood Fleming
Lectures in Southern History

Louisiana State University

Mind and the American Civil War

Mind and the American Civil War

A Meditation on Lost Causes

Lewis P. Simpson

Louisiana State University Press
Baton Rouge and London

Copyright © 1989 by Louisiana State University Press
All rights reserved
Manufactured in the United States of America

Designer: Albert Crochet
Typeface: Linotron Trump Mediaeval
Typesetter: G & S Typesetters, Inc.
Printer: Thomson-Shore, Inc.
Binder: John H. Dekker & Sons, Inc.

First printing
98 97 96 95 94 93 92 91 90 89   5 4 3 2 1

LIBRARY OF CONGRESS CATALOGING-IN-PUBLICATION DATA

Simpson, Lewis P.
    Mind and the American Civil War: a meditation on lost causes /
Lewis P. Simpson.
        p.   cm. — (The Walter Lynwood Fleming lectures in southern
history)
    Includes index.
    ISBN 0-8071-1555-X (alk. paper)
    1. United States—History—Civil War, 1861–1865—Influence.
2. Nationalism—United States—History.   3. Slavery—United States.
I. Title.   II. Series.
E468.9.S57   1989
973.7—dc19   89-30159
                                                        CIP

"Slavery and the Cultural Imperialism of New England" appeared in
the *Southern Review*, n.s., XXV (Winter, 1986).

The paper in this book meets the guidelines for permanence and
durability of the Committee on Production Guidelines for
Book Longevity of the Council on Library Resources. ∞

For
Charles and Sarah East
Fabian and Almena Gudas
Darwin and Leora Shrell
Otis Wheeler
   and,
in affectionate memory,
Doris Wheeler

The brain is wider than the sky,
   For, put them side by side,
The one the other will include
   With ease, and you beside.

The brain is deeper than the sea,
   For, hold them, blue to blue,
The one the other will absorb,
   As sponges, buckets do.

The brain is just the weight of God,
   For, lift them, pound for pound,
And they will differ, if they do,
   As syllable from sound.

—EMILY DICKINSON (ca. 1862: the year of
the Seven Days' Battles, Second Bull Run,
Antietam, and Fredericksburg)

Contents

Preface

❦

Outside of necessary revisions, and some slight amplification, this volume presents the 1988 Walter Lynwood Fleming Lectures in Southern History as they were read in the lecture room. I count the invitation from the distinguished Department of History of Louisiana State University to give the Fleming Lectures as a singular honor. Not only did the invitation come to a member of a literary rather than a history faculty, but it came for the first time to a member of the LSU faculty. Whatever the meaning of these facts may be, it is insignificant compared to the honor of being asked to join the brilliant company of Fleming Lecturers, who have, from the inauguration of the series in 1937 by Charles W. Ramsdell, explored the multifaceted aspects of the history of the American South in its relation to our national history. My own small contribution to this lengthy dialogue represents a brief effort to augment, and in a sense to sum up, my inquiries into a subject I have more or less consistently pursued in the study of American literary and cultural history: the complex, fateful, even tragic connection between the South and New England.

Even though it is a small book, *Mind and the American Civil War* reflects an indebtedness to lives and minds far too numerous for specification. Let me simply express my general gratitude to the LSU Department of History and my particular gratitude to those LSU colleagues who were most immediately involved in the circumstances that brought the work into being. They include John L. Loos, Alumni Professor and chairman, emeritus, of the Department of His-

tory; William J. Cooper, Jr., professor of history and until recently dean of the Graduate School; and Charles W. Royster,
T. Harry Williams Professor of History. I must further thank
other members of the history faculty who have had a helpful
interest in my work, including Burl L. Noggle, Alumni Professor of History, and Professors Anne Loveland and Daniel C.
Littlefield. I am constantly aware, I must add, of the career
and thought of the late T. Harry Williams in shaping my
sense of the drama of the American civil conflict of the
1860s and its meaning as one of the crucial wars of modern
history. Save for John R. May, the present chairman of the
Department of English, I will not, for lack of space, attempt
to single out my many helpful colleagues in the Department
of English. Beyond the campus faculty, two names must be
mentioned. Let me thank Eugene Genovese, who, while he
was serving as Mellon Professor at Tulane University in
1986, provided the impetus for the initial development of
the first part of *Mind and the American Civil War* by invit-
ing me to participate in the Mellon Symposium at Tulane.
And at this point let me also thank Ernest Gaines, writer-in-
residence at the University of Southwestern Louisiana, who
made a special trip to Baton Rouge to join James Olney and
Charles W. Royster in introducing me to the cordial audi-
ences who attended the 1988 Fleming series.

By this time, my debt to Leslie Phillabaum, Beverly Jarrett,
and Margaret Dalrymple of the LSU Press is beyond redemption. I am equally in debt, both personally and profes-
sionally, to the persons to whom this volume is dedicated.
I am now, too, under solid obligation to Maxie Wells of the
staff of the *Henry James Review*. Not only has she patiently
put several versions of my manuscript through the word pro-
cessor, but she has given each one skillful and thoughtful
editorial attention. At the same time, I must express the
most genuine appreciation to Evelyn Heck of the *Southern
Review* staff for her indispensable assistance to me in all my
projects. The enabling center of my work has been Mimi,
my wife and constant companion for all these years.

Mind and the American Civil War

I
Land, Slaves, and Mind: The High Culture of the Jeffersonian South

Intellectual aristocrat and austere moralist, whose career as an American essayist bridged the period from the 1890s to the 1930s, John Jay Chapman was a New Yorker who became a late-blooming spiritual New Englander, his conversion having been brought about by the experience of living in the Boston-Cambridge community as a student at Harvard during the "Indian summer" of the New England Renaissance when Ralph Waldo Emerson was still a visible presence. Although he was an old man suffering from senility, the philosopher was invested in the youthful New Yorker's vision with an aura of sublime light, this deriving, as Chapman says, not only from the symbolic quality of Emerson's renowned selfhood but from his representation of a culture that had had "a consecutive development of thought since colonial times." "One-sided, sad, and inexpressive in many ways," the Boston-Cambridge culture yet exemplified, Chapman observed, what his native city completely lacked. It had "coherence." Boston was not "a railway station" but "a civilization." Its character, on the one hand, reflected its origin in the spiritual and intellectual bonding of a people chosen of God, and, on the other, the connection of this people with that broad "treasury of human thought and experience which flows down out of antiquity and involves us, surrounds us and supports us."[1]

1. John Jay Chapman, "Emerson," in Edmund Wilson (ed.), *The Shock of Recognition: The Development of Literature in the United States Recorded by the Men Who Made It* (New York, 1943), 596–97. Chapman's remarks about Boston are quoted in Wilson's prefatory remarks to the essay on Emerson.

Chapman, in other words, envisioned a seventeenth-century New England that had been not simply an expression of the Reformation culture of dissent but of the high culture of the European Renaissance. Conceiving that, with the passing of time, New England thought, merging the sacred and profane, had become an expression of the high secular culture of Western civilization in the eighteenth and nineteenth centuries, Chapman recognized both the New England of the Transcendentalists—of Emerson, Henry Thoreau, Margaret Fuller, and Theodore Parker—and the New England whose writers and scholars, in the two or three generations before he had come to Harvard, had entered into the lists with European intellectuals and made the Boston world into a cosmopolitan literary culture. This was the intellectual world in which Emerson had proclaimed the arrival of the "American Scholar," Thoreau had written *Walden,* and Margaret Fuller had written *Woman in the Nineteenth Century.* But it was also the world in which the European scientist Louis Agassiz had made his home and founded the Harvard Museum of Comparative Zoology; Henry Wadsworth Longfellow had translated Dante; and John Lothrop Motley had immersed himself in an unprecedented inquiry into the history of the Netherlands. In short, this was the world that had found an archetypal figure not only in an eccentric like Thoreau but also, as Emerson says in "Historic Notes of Life and Letters in New England," in a scholar like George Ticknor. Author of a monumental history of Spanish literature, Ticknor had in 1815 inaugurated the study of modern languages and literature in the United States by becoming the first New Englander to enter a German university with the intention of becoming a student of modern rather than classical literature.

It would not have occurred to Chapman, in any positive sense at least, that there could have been any connection between the character of the ambitious high culture of nineteenth-century New England and the culture of the detestable slave society that existed "at the South" before, as

Chapman termed it, "our most blessed war."[2] That in actuality the tie was profound we need only to recall the intellectual history of the Revolutionary age as this is exemplified
in Thomas Jefferson and John Adams. But at this point, pick-
ing up on Chapman's remark about the coherence of the
New England culture, I want to mention in particular another relationship, that between Jefferson and George Ticknor, this being more pointedly relevant to certain ironies in
the antebellum intellectual relationship between the South
and New England that I propose briefly to explore. It will become apparent as I go on, in fact, that I see the Ticknor-
Jefferson connection in the context of a broader relationship:
that between Jefferson and Ralph Waldo Emerson. Born in
1803, Emerson, who was just beginning a career in the Boston pulpit when Jefferson died in 1826, was apparently unknown to Jefferson, but he was to be the only New England
intellectual prior to the Civil War who has an importance in
American literary and intellectual history comparable to
that of Jefferson.

In 1814, after he graduated from Harvard, Ticknor, a Bostonian's Bostonian—who not only instituted the study of
modern languages and literatures at Harvard, but was the
principal founder of the Boston Public Library—made an unprecedented decision about his future. Instead of electing to
become a minister, a lawyer, or possibly a teacher of the clas-
sics, he announced that he would reverse the time-sanctioned
mandate that a young gentleman supplement his education
in books by a trip abroad to study men and manners. In his
own case, Ticknor roundly declared, he would spend three or
four years in Europe pursuing an education derived from
"not men, but books."[3] How seriously he took this prime intention was indicated by the purpose of Ticknor's first European sojourn, a period of subjection to the austere discipline

2. *Ibid.*, 654.
3. Ticknor to N. A. Haven, July, 1814, in *Life, Letters and Journals of
George Ticknor*, ed. George S. Hilliard and Anna Eliot Ticknor (2 vols.;
Boston, 1876), I, 23.

of the German scholars at Göttingen. Although the portrayal of men and women in his letters offers convincing, and delightful, proof that he hardly stuck to his intention to study only books, Ticknor—moving eventually from Göttingen to Paris to Rome to Spain and finally to England—kept to his chief purpose with Puritan firmness and laid the basis for the whole of his scholarly career.

But the fixity of his resolve may not be ascribed altogether, perhaps not even primarily, to his New England heritage. The scholar whose advice about letters and learning in Europe he had most eagerly sought during a period of diligent preparation for his sojourn abroad lived far away from the Boston-Cambridge literati on Carter's Mountain near Charlottesville, Virginia. Indeed, in his search for advice from American men of letters as to "in what parts of the countries I mean to visit I can most easily compass my objects," Ticknor desired to visit Monticello as the climax of his American preparation for Europe.[4] In a way, this was a somewhat perverse desire. A meeting with Jefferson was hardly an easy matter. For one thing, it was awkward politically, since, although not given to militant politics, Ticknor was by the sympathies of family and class firmly attached to the Federalist remnant in New England, who still regarded the author of the Embargo Act with distrust if not acrimony. For another thing, a journey to Charlottesville was difficult and at times hazardous.

Nonetheless, after visiting with two other Virginians— the acerbic John Randolph, who was temporarily residing in Philadelphia, and President James Madison—Ticknor (armed with a letter of introduction from John Adams, who only a year or so earlier had had a reconciliation with Jefferson) left a desolate national capital that had lately been burned by the British troops in February, 1815, for a week-long journey through Virginia. Enduring hardships that, he told his father, might match his own "sufferings as a Revolutionary sol-

4. *Ibid.*, I, 23.

dier," Ticknor found himself on a Saturday morning one week later traveling the short distance from Charlottesville to Jefferson's mountain, where he made a winding "ascent of this steep, savage hill, as pensive and slow as Satan's ascent to Paradise."[5]

The long weekend he spent at Jefferson's fabled plantation seat included two mornings, at the former president's invitation, inspecting his "collection of books." This library, "now so much talked about," was, Ticknor learned, made up of "about seven thousand volumes contained in a suite of fine rooms," and arranged "in the catalogue, and on the shelves, according to the divisions and subdivisions of human learning by Lord Bacon." In addition to the time he spent with Jefferson in the company of the table, Ticknor had two hours with him in the privacy of his study, during which "the old philosopher" told him about his own experience of Europe and offered on a "month's notice" to supply a list of his friends and correspondents abroad, though he added sadly that the number had been considerably diminished by death. As Ticknor took his leave of Monticello the next day, Jefferson reminded him several times about "writing for letters to his friends in Europe."[6]

Literature and learning having prevailed over politics, Ticknor and Jefferson began a cordial acquaintanceship. As Jefferson advanced toward the realization at long last of his scheme to establish the University of Virginia—an institution he had already envisioned in 1800 as being so "broad & liberal & *modern*, as to be worth patronizing with the public support"—Ticknor, now the Smith Professor of the French and Spanish Languages and Literatures and Professor of Belles-Lettres at Harvard, welcomed the prospect of a new American university to serve as a rival to a moribund Harvard. When the prospect of "Mr. Jefferson's University" was made a reality by the Virginia legislature, Ticknor enter-

5. See letters from Ticknor to Elisha Ticknor, January 6, 17, 21, 26, 1815, all *ibid.*, I, 27–30, 31–33.
6. See Ticknor to Elisha Ticknor, February 7, 1815, *ibid.*, I, 34–38.

tained Jefferson's urgent invitation to accept the professorship of belles-lettres (salary: two thousand dollars and a
campus residence). But even though Ticknor, who was beginning to feel thoroughly frustrated by the problems of
modernizing the curriculum at Harvard, viewed the University of Virginia as "the first truly liberal establishment for
the highest branches of education, that has been attempted
in this country," he declined the offer to move to Charlottesville. His interest in the University of Virginia nonetheless
remained keen; and a little later on, the invitation to join
the Virginia faculty still open, he visited Jefferson once again,
and with the founder himself as guide toured the "academi-
cal village" devised by the architectural genius of Jefferson.
The magnificent library constructed in the likeness of the
Pantheon, the bright lecture halls, and the attractive student
quarters and faculty residences were, in Ticknor's estimation, "more beautiful than anything architectural in New
England, and more appropriate to an university than can be
found, perhaps, in the world." His buildings, Ticknor believed, were admirably adapted to Jefferson's radical scheme
of combining classical and modern disciplines and allowing
students to elect a course of study in one of eight "schools":
moral philosophy, mathematics, natural history, natural
philosophy, law, anatomy and medicine, ancient languages,
and modern languages.[7]

Yet in spite of his admiration for Jefferson and his new university, Ticknor was not lured to Charlottesville. In the light
of his resentment of the resistance he was encountering in
his efforts to entice Harvard to join the nineteenth century—eventually this would lead to his resignation from the
Harvard faculty—we may wonder why Ticknor did not make
the move. No doubt his reasons for not doing so included the
fact that he was an urban-oriented intellectual. Even though
Boston was still small, it was by American standards a city.

---

7. David B. Tyack, *George Ticknor and the Boston Brahmins* (Cambridge, Mass., 1967), 103.

It was, moreover, a major port on the Atlantic, from whence Ticknor could readily embark for Europe when he wished. He could hardly have imagined himself contentedly settling down in a remote village whether in Virginia or Massachusetts. But a deeper motive in Ticknor's rejection of a position at the new institution, in spite of the fact that it promised him freedom from the intellectual backwardness of Harvard, was, I would conjecture, that the cosmopolitan Ticknor paradoxically could not really imagine himself taking up permanent residence in any place save his native city, not even in Paris, Madrid, or London. He had no wish to go into exile, and this is what leaving Boston permanently, whether for Charlottesville or Paris, would have meant to him.

Ironically, it would have meant exile in a more complete sense if he had taken up residence in Charlottesville than if he had done so in a European metropolis. We realize this, I think, when we consider the other side of the Ticknor-Jefferson relationship; for if Ticknor had no inclination to live in any place other than Boston, the even more cosmopolitan Jefferson had no real inclination to live anywhere except at Monticello, not even in a city he loved like Paris. We cannot even remotely imagine Jefferson, had he somehow been invited to assume a professorship at Harvard, exiling himself in Boston and Cambridge.

Describing the ironic parochialism of a New England cosmopolite and a Virginia cosmopolite, I am adducing a good deal from unspoken attitudes we may attribute to Ticknor and Jefferson, hoping to invoke the inarticulate ironies of the culture of mind in Massachusetts and Virginia in the third decade of the new nation—ironies that may seem humorous or trivial, or both, yet which lie close to the center of the inner history of the American Republic as this began to unfold by 1820 with the relentless progress of a Greek tragedy. Or maybe I should employ a different analogy and say, with the tangled progress of the tragicomedy of Shakespeare.

In any event, the developing character of the American

drama revealed itself in the ironic difference between Jefferson's idealistic proclamation in 1820 that the University of
Virginia would become a "bulwark of the human mind in
the western hemisphere" and his dire warning about the future of the Republic only a year later, when the meaning of
the struggle over the extension of slavery into Missouri
seemed like a "firebell in the night." In a letter to a member
of the Virginia legislature, Jefferson urged that the University of Virginia be opened as soon as possible, for it was
needed to fulfill the "holy charge" of inculcating young
minds with the principles of Virginia. I quote directly from
Jefferson's letter:

> I learn, with deep affliction, that nothing is likely to be done
> for our University this year. . . . I had hoped . . . that we should
> open with the next year an institution on which the fortunes of
> our country may depend more than may meet the general eye.
> The reflections that the boys of this age are to be the men of the
> next; that they should be prepared to receive the holy charge
> which we are cherishing to deliver over to them; that in estab-
> lishing an institution of wisdom for them, we secure it to all our
> future generations; that in fulfilling this duty, we bring home to
> our own bosoms the sweet consolation of seeing our sons rising
> under a luminous tuition, to destinies of high promise; these are
> considerations which will occur to all; but all, I fear, do not see
> the speck in our horizon which is to burst on us as a tornado,
> sooner or later. The line of division lately marked out between
> different portions of our confederacy, is such as will never, I fear,
> be obliterated, and we are not trusting to those who are against
> us in position and principle, to fashion to their own form the
> minds and affections of our youth. If, as has been estimated, we
> send three hundred thousand dollars a year to the northern semi-
> naries, for the instruction of our own sons, then we must have
> there five hundred of our sons, imbibing opinions and principles
> in discord with those of their own country. This canker is eating
> on the vitals of our existence, and if not arrested at once, will be
> beyond remedy.[8]

8. Jefferson to Thomas Cooper, August 14, 1820, Jefferson to James
Breckenridge, February 15, 1821, both in *Writings of Thomas Jefferson*, ed.
Andrew A. Lipscomb and Albert Ellery Bergh (20 vols.; Washington, D.C.,
1905), XV, 269, 314–15.

In itself, neither this letter nor, for that matter, Jefferson's explicit identification of Harvard in another comment as an institution particularly antagonistic to southern principles, indicates attitudes that in themselves would have been objectionable to Ticknor. Nor would Ticknor have been concerned about the fact that Jefferson was deliberately seeking faculty members for his university who, like Jefferson, would be at once free thinkers about religion and "safe" on the slavery question. Ticknor was far from being an abolitionist. Nurtured in the bosom of a strict New England Federalism, he was committed to the ultra Whiggism that refused the moralism of the "conscience Whigs" and defended Websterian constitutionalism. Ticknor, moreover, subscribed to the Jeffersonian, and arch Whig, conviction that the inferiority of the Negro as a species of human being had been scientifically verified; and that, although slavery was a curse, it was to be abolished only through colonization. Actually by the 1850s Ticknor became somewhat paranoiac about slavery, and said that if the colonization effort could not be accomplished, the African slaves in America were doomed to extermination in an inevitable war with the superior Anglo-Saxon race. When the Civil War came, he was suspected in some quarters of being a secessionist because he declared that Lincoln and the Republicans had transformed the presidency into a dictatorship and that the war was being fought at the expense of constitutional government.

Yet in spite of his prosouthern attitudes, Ticknor had no thought of deserting New England. He was a cultural ideologue who believed that the truth of the American Republic, not to say truth in the largest sense possible, was invested in New England, particularly in eastern Massachusetts. In his view, New England would always purify itself of the errors it might make at any given time. Given his sensitivity to the culture of New England, Ticknor could hardly have failed to feel a certain incompatibility with Jefferson, particularly under the pressures dramatically signaled by the Missouri Compromise. After this event, he could not have failed to

recognize that the cosmopolitan idealist he had met at Monticello in 1815 represented an opposing cultural ideology,
which held that the truth of the Republic, and truth generally, had been invested not in New England but in the South,
notably in eastern Virginia. Ticknor could hardly have subscribed to Jefferson's suspicion that southern students attending institutions of learning in the North, notably Harvard,
were deliberately being instructed in "anti-Missourism" and
other doctrines subversive of the principles of true freedom—principles that had once, Jefferson thought, been accepted by all American citizens but were now, he feared, re-
spected only in the southern states.

In the increasing tendency of New Englanders to doubt the
motives of southerners and vice versa, we detect a falling off
from the transcendent moral and intellectual context of the
mind that had made the American Revolution. At Monticello in 1815, in the pre–Missouri Compromise age, it was
possible for Ticknor to believe that he was encountering
Jefferson in a polity other than that of the struggling infant
Republic of the United States. Everywhere about him were
evidences of Jefferson's self-conscious representation of the
life-style that Ticknor longed to emulate—that of the citizen
of the polity which, Voltaire exulted in the mid-eighteenth
century, had defied wars and religious persecutions to spread
everywhere and everywhere to become independent; a polity
that Jefferson himself in 1811, in the midst of the ecumeni-
cal slaughter of the Napoleonic years, had confirmed yet to
exist as "a great fraternity spreading over the whole earth."[9]

This was the realm that had come into existence during the process of the secularization of mind in the West—
when, as far back as the thirteenth century, predecessors of
the Renaissance humanists began to sense that whatever
their relation to the realms of church and state, they lived
also in another realm of existence, distinct from the realms
both of the king and the universal church (or "the republic of

9. Jefferson to John Hollins, February 19, 1809, *ibid.*, XII, 253.

Christ"). This was the first modern republic, the republic of letters. By the sixteenth and seventeenth centuries, the polity of letters was represented not so much by the university, which had been a part of the ecclesiastical realm, as in the academies, salons, and the extensive correspondence of the literary and learned. By the end of the seventeenth century, when printing presses became omnipresent, the republic of letters began to be conceived as universally embodied in the ever-increasing number of books and periodicals. This great polity of secular mind had become the agency of a postmedieval, post-Christendom critique of God and man, nature and society, and, not less, mind itself. Culminating in Descartes, Bacon, Newton, and Locke, in Voltaire, Rousseau, Diderot, and Vico, the great critique not only destroyed the European hierarchical society of myth and tradition but ruthlessly transferred God and nature, man and society, and mind itself, into mind. In this process of moving all that is into the human mind—a process that would now seem to be irreversible even though it may result in the destruction of the world—we define the high culture of modernity and discover the determinative movement of modern history: the ineluctable reduction of every transcendent reference point of history—the eternal republic of Platonic conception, the eternal city of Augustinian vision, the images and icons of both church and state, all the trappings of tradition—to historical relics, this by the unending desire, the unending will, of the human mind to put itself into the possession both of the natural universe and of human history.[10]

When Ticknor walked into Monticello in 1815, he found that one wall of the entrance hall was embellished with various "curiosities" from the "wild and perilous expedition" of Lewis and Clark, while, "in odd union," another wall dis-

10. The initial part of this study is an attempt to refine and to a degree refocus certain broad theses developed elsewhere. See especially Lewis P. Simpson, *The Brazen Face of History: Studies in the Literary Consciousness in America* (Baton Rouge, 1980); Lewis P. Simpson, "Jefferson and the Writing of the South," in *Columbia Literary History of the United States,* ed. Emory Eliott (New York, 1987), 128–35.

played a "fine painting of the Repentance of Saint Peter"
and "an Indian map on leather, of the southern waters of
the Missouri." Going into the drawing room, Ticknor beheld
a picture of the "Laughing and Weeping Philosophers," dividing the world between them, and a copy of Raphael's
"Transfiguration," along with "portraits of Madison in the
plain, Quaker-like dress of his youth, Lafayette in his Revolutionary uniform, and Franklin in the dress in which we always see him." In a very real sense, at Monticello the future
American historian of Spanish culture had arrived in a place
that at once symbolized the realm of letters, learning, and
art, and the great modern motive: the transference of world,
God, and man into mind. He stood in a place that—directly
reflecting the mind of its architect and builder, a man who
had spent his life making a nation that he said had no model
in the parchment records of feudal tradition but was an invention of the modern mind—was in itself a concentrated
symbol of the unalterable movement of modern history, the
movement into mind.

Within a year and a half after Ticknor had made his second
journey to Virginia, this time to see Jefferson's dream university being actualized in wood and brick, the founder had departed the scene, having with eminent appropriateness died
on the same day as John Adams, July 4, 1826. For the nation,
the regions, and the states to which they were so deeply attached, the passing of each of these makers of the Republic
was freighted with symbolic meaning. This tends to become
obscured, I must remark, if too much emphasis is placed on
the reconciling correspondence between Jefferson and Adams
during the last twelve years or so before they died. A great
human and political drama—one of the greatest records of
the passions and issues of the American Revolution—the
Jefferson-Adams letters yet bear the impress of an ineffable
nostalgia. In a letter written toward the end of the correspondence, Adams said, "I look back with rapture to those golden
days when Virginia and Massachusetts lived and acted together like a band of brothers and I hope it may not be long

before they say redeunt saturnia regna."[11] But the dream of a golden age is always a dream of what never was and never is to be. The death of Adams—the latter-day Puritan, who, someone has said, was a philosophe in spite of himself—represented the end of a career that had exemplified in New England the phenomenon in modern Western cultural history that Hegel called the secularization of the spiritual. More particularly, in the history of the New England culture—or more particularly still in the history of the culture of Massachusetts—Adams' career had reflected the culmination of what has been described as a logical, coherent transition from the culture of a prescriptive theocratic society to that of a capitalistic, putatively free, and—in its own interpretation of itself—strongly moral society. The death of Jefferson, on the other hand, marked the end of a career that logically should have embodied—and often has been regarded as actually embodying—the achievement of a fully definitive stage in the secularization of a culture that even at the time of its transplantation to America, in contrast to the theocratic culture of New England, had reached a comparatively advanced stage of economic adventurism and intellectual freedom.

Yet in its inner history the career of Jefferson represents the frustration of the very achievement it has been said so notably to signify. To put this another way, Jefferson's death occurred at almost the point when the liberalism we associate with his Virginia lost its coherent thrust toward fulfillment. This may be attributed not only to the depletion of the Virginia soil by excessive tobacco cultivation but to the inhibiting awareness of the relationship of slavery to mind. Such an awareness was not suddenly formed in the early 1820s as a response to the Missouri Compromise and the development of the abolitionist agitation. The confrontation between mind and slavery is implicit in Jefferson's whole career. But

11. Lester J. Cappon (ed.), *The Adams-Jefferson Letters: The Complete Correspondence Between Thomas Jefferson and Abigail and John Adams* (2 vols.; Chapel Hill, 1959), II, 610.

since the man of "sobriety and cool reason" whom Ticknor encountered at Monticello habitually wore the Enlightenment mask—the bland, quiet "smile of reason"—the complexity of his mind is more difficult to discern than that of his intellectual peers Franklin and Voltaire, who constantly articulated their sense of the ironic relation between knowledge and society. The man of letters who wrote the Declaration of Independence and never ceased to denounce slavery—yet in his lifetime never freed any of the numerous slaves he owned (save two, one of whom bought his freedom)—has been interpreted as bearing a likeness to such children of the Enlightenment as Thomas Paine, Condorcet, or Voltaire's fictional Pangloss. But Jefferson was scarcely so simple as these un-ironic optimists. Reading him closely, one suspects that he had a sense of irony but deliberately suppressed it in implicit obedience to the culture of which he was an integral part—the culture of an evolving slave society that paradoxically conceived itself to be an integral part of the expansion of the modern polity of the free mind. I cannot elaborate how this is so in detail, but let me attempt to suggest a historical rationale for the culture of mind in Virginia.

By the seventeenth century, the disposition of the English aristocracy and gentry in creating an alliance between governance and mind had produced educated, self-conscious, self-reflective upper-class men of letters in the manorial establishment who were committed to the perpetuation of the traditional order against the forces that would destroy it, Puritan or otherwise. But making a self-conscious effort to perpetuate order is quite different from the unthinking assumption of a given mode of life as an inherent condition of existence. Tradition in its manifestation in the feudal society of icon and ritual, of hierarchy and reciprocal duty, in a society that assumes the patriarchal family as its model, was displaced when it became an object of preservation. Becoming something that must be deliberately conserved, it became, in other words, a mental construct. Commenting on

the development of the modern relation between traditionalism and conservative desire to perpetuate the past, Karl
Mannheim said: "The simple habit of living more or less unconsciously, as though the old ways of life were still appropriate, gradually gives way to a deliberate effort to maintain
them under new conditions, and they are raised to the level
of conscious 'reflection.'" Thereby, Mannheim adds, "conservative thought . . . saves itself . . . by raising to the level
of reflection and conscious manipulation those forms of experience which can no longer be had in an authentic way."[12]
To be more exact, one must say that this is not how conservative thought "saves itself" so much as how in the first
place it comes into existence, this being by mind's willed displacement in itself of the "authentic" experience of tradition.
An assumed way of life, in other words, displaced by history,
is converted by mind into an idea of this life. Weighted with
emotion, the idea may elevate a way of life that, as we say,
has become historical into the status of an ideal way of life,
or, to be more precise, into an ideology.

How can the traditional society be preserved as the model
of the right conduct of mind in the face of the modern shift
to the vision of mind as the proper model of society? This
may only be accomplished, to be sure, by mind's assertion
that society is its model. That this is in effect what happens
is prominently witnessed by the emergence in seventeenth-
century England of a learned, self-conscious, highly articulate intellectual traditionalist like Sir Robert Filmer, whose
best-known book, *Patriarcha* (not published until 1680 but
written at the time of the outbreak of the Puritan rebellion

12. Karl Mannheim, "The Meaning of Conservatism," in *Essays on Sociology and Social Psychology* (London, 1953), 115. I am indebted for this
reference to Professor Susan Donaldson, who has also called my attention
to the independent development of a similar thesis by John Shelton Reed
in "For Dixieland: The Sectionalism of *I'll Take My Stand*," in *A Band
of Prophets: The Vanderbilt Agrarians After Fifty Years*, ed. William C.
Havard and Walter Sullivan (Baton Rouge, 1982), 41–64. My own essay in
this volume, I might add, is also relevant: "The Southern Republic of
Letters and *I'll Take My Stand*," *ibid.*, 65–91.

and circulated in manuscript for the edification of his fellow
gentry in Kent), argues that the true basis of order is not the
monarchy but the patriarchal family structure, with its intricate network of cousinage, that Filmer knew on the manorial estates of Kent. Significantly, the Filmerian thesis became a classic statement of social doctrine only because of
John Locke's widely published opposition to it a generation
later in the development of his contractual theory of the ori-
gins of government. Filmer, the patriarch as man of letters—
in an articulate recovery of a way of life that was dying—had
created a relation between mind and land essentially different from the connection that had existed between the unlet-
tered and inarticulate feudal lord and his dominion. He in-
ternalized land and dominion over it as a historical concept.
Locke's opposition to this concept revealed the ironic character of Filmer's role: the traditionalist who is not only a
moral theorist but the self-conscious interpreter of history.

Meanwhile, as the English historian Peter Laslett has observed, even as Filmer became the theorist of patriarchalism, something was happening to the Kentish cousinage. It
began to extend itself across the Atlantic to Virginia. Actually, the initial stage of the Kentish participation in the Virginia settlement goes back to the very founding in 1606 of
the Virginia Company of London, which numbered among
its sponsors, officers, and seamen several persons with important Kentish connections, including the company trea-
surer, George Sandys (who was to make a noted translation
of Ovid in the Virginia wilderness). But it was not until
1619—when the Virginia Company granted a patent "unto
sundry Kentishmen, who would seate and plant themselves
in Virginia" in exchange for "large priviledges and immu-
nities"—that the colony began to develop a Kentish core.
This expanded as the younger sons of Kentish families came
to Virginia to seek opportunities denied them in their native
place, and it increased substantially when the civil war of
1640–60 made refugees out of some members of a Kentish

cousinage that had roots in Dorset, Sussex, and Essex: Washingtons, Randolphs, Carters, Culpeppers, Lees, Byrds, Fitzhughs, and Masons.

The story of the early Virginia planters' families [Laslett says] illustrates the most important feature of the English gentry of the time—the immense strength of the family bond and the extraordinary cohesion of the grouping of families by locality. There could be no more vivid illustration of patriarchalism at work. It is quite impossible to single out one strand of surnames from the network of affiliation which grew up as generation succeeded generation. It so happens that the bloc of families in which we are interested [the Kentish] became involved in Virginia colonization at the outset. It followed as a simple consequence that the whole network, not an individual strand, should reproduce itself in the colony within a generation.

The "most characteristic thing" the seventeenth-century gentry of Kent produced, Laslett concludes, "was the political thinking of Sir Robert Filmer and the most surprising was the society of the Old South in the United States."[13] Discounting an oversimplified generalization, we may at the same time emphasize a major implication of Filmer's thought that Laslett does not bring into focus. This is simply the fact that in becoming the theorist of patriarchalism (and the chosen opponent of John Locke) Filmer like Locke effectively became a citizen of the intellectual community of the high culture of the eighteenth century. A generation later, the significance of the Filmerian image of the patriarch as man of letters was further enhanced when the descendants of the Kentish migration to the southern colonies, the plantation patriarchs of Virginia, joining land and chattel slavery to mind, created a novel version of the man of letters—that is to say, the man of letters as plantation patriarch and chat-

13. Peter Laslett, "The Gentry of Kent in 1640," in T. H. Breen (ed.), *Shaping Southern Society: The Colonial Experience* (New York, 1975), 45–46. See also Gordon J. Schochet, *Patriarchalism in Political Thought: The Authoritarian Family and Political Speculation and Attitudes, Especially in Seventeenth-Century England* (New York, 1975).

tel slave master. This generation of lettered Virginians denied the antagonism between Filmer and Locke and based a revolution substantially on Lockean theory.

But judging from the records of their lives, what to us today may well seem the graphic historical irony of this situation was largely lost on those who were intimately a part of it. The major case in point is Jefferson.

Governed by the inclination of his time and place, of his culture, to associate the possibilities of mind and letters with the figure of the plantation master, Jefferson was so thoroughly a member of the plantation patriciate that, although he publicly opposed slavery all his long life, he never even remotely imagined altering his own social status as a way of authenticating his opposition. The earliest memory he had was of being carried on a silk pillow by a slave; he built Monticello with slave labor; he staffed his elegant household with slaves; he was carried to his grave on the slope below his mansion in a slave-built coffin. Monticello and its master constituted the culminating image of an equation of land, slaves, and mind that had been evolving in the southern planting society for at least two generations before Jefferson.

This is not to claim, I should hasten to say, that the pre-Jeffersonian man of letters was exclusively embodied in the figure of the planter. One must take carefully into account such figures as Dr. Alexander Hamilton, the physician who founded the Tuesday Club in Annapolis; the Reverend Hugh Jones and the Reverend William Stith, both historians of Virginia; William Parks, noted founder of the *Virginia Gazette*; and of course the famed lawyer Patrick Henry. But the figures of the unlanded clergyman or printer or lawyer on the whole counted for less in the southern than in the northern colonies. The man of power in the South was represented in figures like William Fitzhugh and Robert Carter. Fitzhugh, who acquired a large estate in Stafford County, Virginia, mixed law and tobacco planting and carried on a personal correspondence that, because of its personal and detailed quality, has been accorded a marked place in colonial letters. Carter—"King Carter" of Cortoman (the name of his Virginia plantation)—lent his plantation seat an aura of the literary and intellectual because of his substantial library of legal, religious, and historical works.

A more complete expression of the relation between letters and the plantation is to be found in the instance of the second Robert Beverley, who left Jamestown and public life in 1706 to take up his residence for the last eighteen years of his life at Beverley Park in King and Queen County, Virginia. Here Beverley, a widower, lived plainly and self-sufficiently. While he directed his slaves and indentured servants in the cultivation of grapes—hoping he could redeem his land from depletion caused by tobacco growing—he enjoyed the pleasures of his library and wrote a classic colonial work, *The History and Present State of Virginia*. A self-conscious inheritor of the Virgilian mode of pastoral, Beverley generates a tension in his history between an almost nostalgic celebration of the beauties and amenities of Virginia when it was inhabited solely by Indians and its degradation by invading tobacco-planting Englishmen. In the light of his literary education, Beverley's motive is predictable and we can ascribe to it no element of originality as such; but in his very adherence to the Virgilian tradition of the man of letters as a moral authority, the master of Beverley Park presents the image of the man of letters in a new guise, that of a Virginia plantation master. In this semblance, an author on a remote plantation on the southern seaboard of the British colonial settlement in America assumes the role of literary authority, presiding over a symbolic extension of the cosmopolitan realm of letters. Reinforced by the career of William Byrd II of Westover, this figure evolved into its representation by the slave masters who rebelled against the authority of king and church: among them, besides Thomas Jefferson, the diarist and pamphleteer Landon Carter of Sabine Hall; the author of the prototype of the Declaration of Independence, the Virginia Bill of Rights, George Mason of Gunston Hall;

the orator and pamphleteer Richard Henry Lee of Chantilly; the political philosopher James Madison of Montpelier; the dramatist Robert Munford of Richland; and the poet St. George Tucker of Matoax.

Why these men of letters and "freedom fighters" were slaveholders is not altogether clear. The obvious reason why chattel slavery became the dominant labor system in most of the southern colonies in the eighteenth century was the need for laborers to work the constantly expanding extent of land being brought under cultivation. As early as 1683 the need was so great that William Byrd I, seeking tobacco to export, found that "without servants or slaves" to trade "no great crop is now to be purchased." Responding to the labor market, traders brought in captive Africans in increasing quantity; and by the second decade of the eighteenth century planters had committed themselves to the slave system, their commitment becoming more absolute when they formed the practice of converting land and chattels into cash when crop or market failed.

But economic expediency was not the only reason slavery became a fixed institution in the southern colonies. More significantly, if Edmund Morgan is correct in *American Slavery/American Freedom: The Ordeal of Colonial Virginia*, planters developed a fateful political stake in slavery. Slavery answered the need to stem the ominous development of a class of free white poor that grew apace in Virginia as laborers bound for a limited term of service were released from indentured status. Unable to transform the indenture system into slavery because it was impolitic to attempt to enslave people of their own race, the Virginia lords solved the problem of the potential insurgency of a mass of freed servants (which they saw as having become reality in Bacon's Rebellion in 1676) by replacing them with laborers whose status as human beings they generally considered to be so inferior that their enslavement required no justification. Pursuing this expediency, though without altogether realizing that they were doing so, those in power in the largest, most populous, and wealthiest southern colony established a society that solved the most vexatious political problem in the Old World, that of poverty.

In discovering the solution to the problem of poverty, the slaveholders of Virginia were not in violation of but in accord with the radical quest of the Enlightenment mind to discover—not in an ideal reference for republican order existing in eternity but in mind itself, in mind's own power to solve social problems—the source and model of freedom; for the leading proponents of the Enlightenment quest, including John Locke, did not envision the principle of the sovereignty of the individual and its corollary, the right of revolution, as extending to the mindless poor. Locke himself, though he had considered the poor to be impediments to freedom, had not advocated their enslavement; but some post-Lockean political theorists, in adapting Locke to an ardent republicanism, specifically urged slavery as a practical means of dealing with the frustration of freedom by poverty. These included eighteenth-century "commonwealth men" like James Burgh and Andrew Fletcher of Saltoun, whose writings Jefferson studied closely. During his time as a law student of George Wythe in Williamsburg in the 1760s, Jefferson, in fact, became thoroughly imbued with the sources of British republican thought. Fletcher, Edmund Morgan points out, had a scheme to enhance the possibilities of freedom in Britain by enslaving two hundred thousand Scotsmen, which was "roughly the number of slaves in Virginia."

It was not feasible to institute such a rational reform in an old society like Scotland's, which still found its image of authority in a transcendently ordered hierarchy, but a society that was coming to regard itself as an invention by the rational mind might plausibly assume that, since independence involved not only freedom from a monarch but from the mob, a productive labor system that eliminates the source of the mob, the inferior and poverty-stricken class, is both eminently reasonable and feasible. The equation of land, mind, and slavery in Virginia was summed up with simplistic yet penetrating clarity by an English traveler who, according to Morgan, said in 1805 that Virginians "can profess an unbounded love of liberty and of democracy in consequence of the mass of the people, who in their countries might become mobs, being there nearly altogether composed of their own Negro slaves."[14]

While the nature and meaning of this attitude can be studied in Washington and other Virginia slave masters and men of letters who were active Revolutionists, we see its fullest realization in Jefferson. Indeed, it is not too much to say that the primary subject of his only book, *Notes on the State of Virginia* (privately printed, 1785; publicly printed, 1787), is by implication the intricate connection between slavery and the rational ethos. Structured as a series of replies to queries about Virginia propounded by François de Barbé-Marbois, secretary of the French legation in Philadelphia, *Notes on Virginia*—which established Jefferson as the archetypal southern man of letters—was the product of hard work during a period of anxious leisure, having been written mostly in 1781–82, the dark time when Jefferson, retired from the governorship, was under investigation because of military reverses in Virginia. Revised and expanded during the next two years, *Notes on Virginia* was not at first intended for publication, and it was not issued in a public printing until six years after the initial draft was finished. Firmly bracketed by an initial chapter on the exact boundaries of Virginia and a final chapter dealing with historical works and documents pertaining to Virginia's "affairs present or ancient," Jefferson's book may give the initial appearance of being a factual account of the geography and history of the state. But its outward form belies the intrinsic purpose of *Notes on Virginia*, which is to conduct an anxious, searching inquiry into the cultural crisis of the author's world.

A deeply personal work, in its way at times a kind of poem, *Notes on Virginia* is a portrayal of the mind of a man of

14. Edmund S. Morgan, *American Slavery/American Freedom: The Ordeal of Virginia* (New York, 1975), 380. See generally, pp. 363–87.

letters under the pressures generated by his divided endeavor
to represent both the ideals of the Enlightenment polity of
letters and the interests of a provincial slave society that
had, without any real intention of abolishing its own slave
system, paradoxically committed itself to the rejection of
slavery to a king in the name of the sovereignty of the self.
Out of the complex tensions in *Notes on Virginia* emerges a
tangled drama of Virginia's historical meaning that em-
braces not only Virginia and the other southern states but
the whole nation. More than the Declaration of Independence, this work symbolizes the enmeshment of Americans
in the energizing historical force of the human mind's will
to power. Yet, unlike the Declaration, *Notes on Virginia* not
only distinctly places in doubt mind's capacity to execute its
will to assume responsibility for history but casts a shadow
on the very validity of mind's conception of itself as the in-
strumentality of reason in history.

Jefferson first mentions slavery in *Notes on Virginia* in the
eighth chapter during a discussion of the relation between
freedom and the demographic character of Virginia. Commenting on the constant movement of agricultural laborers
from the continent of Europe, where land is scarce and labor
abundant, to a world where labor is scarce and land abundant, he expresses a fear of the further intrusion into Virginia of foreigners from countries governed by "absolute
monarchies." Such immigrants may threaten prospects for
harmony and durability in a society based on "specific principles" of government that, "derived from the freest principles of the English constitution" and from "natural right
and natural reason," are "more peculiar than those of any
other in the universe." Jefferson's stress on the absolute sin-
gularity of a society that has joined British principles of freedom to those inherent in nature implies that he saw the
nation that was coming into being—as represented in particular by the state of Virginia—as a historically unique
instance of freedom. This implication is intensified in the
conclusion of the eighth chapter, when Jefferson tacitly re-

lates the problem of controlling the influx of immigrants to America from absolutist societies to that of controlling the importation of slaves. Concluding that, because of the natural increase of the slave population under the beneficent treatment of slaves in Virginia, the proportion of free to slave has become only eleven to ten, Jefferson applauds an act of the General Assembly that would inhibit the growth of slavery by banning forever the transportation of slaves into the state from beyond the national boundaries. "This will," he says, "in some measure stop the increase of this great political and moral evil, while the minds of our citizens may be ripening for a complete emancipation of human nature."[15]

We may well be given pause by this bland, apparently guileless conjecture. What is the import of Jefferson's implied radical dissociation of mind from nature? Suggesting that the moral power of the human mind will eventually be sufficient to redeem human nature from its disposition to evil, does Jefferson simply make the idealistic suggestion—contradicting his subscription to the view that blacks are inherently inferior—that mind (the superior minds of Virginians, or Americans) will ripen into a state of moral perfection, and that in this perfected state, recognizing that all men are by nature human beings, will cease to consider slaves as essentially nonhuman creatures, recognize them as moral and intellectual equals, and accept humanity as one? Or does Jefferson offer the radical suggestion that, having achieved the state of moral perfection, the human mind in its superior manifestations will emancipate itself from its ancient inherence in the physical and psychological limitations of human nature and part company with it forever? Is Jefferson making the awesome prophecy that in emancipating the slaves the human mind will unite the will to freedom and the will to power—that in doing so mind will achieve its emancipation from history? Jefferson, we are reminded, lived in the age when Mary Shelley wrote *Frankenstein.*

15. *Notes on the State of Virginia,* in *Thomas Jefferson: Writings,* ed. Merrill D. Peterson; Library of America edition (New York, 1984), 211, 214.

Jefferson's projection of the end of slavery under the auspicious conditions of thought in America is—is it not?—a kind of metaphor for America as the representation in history of the Cartesian severance of mind and body; of America as the triumphant incarnation of the secular, rational will to take not only society but the universe into itself. Yet Jefferson's assurance of mind's capacity masks an intense vexation that haunts subsequent chapters of *Notes on Virginia*, especially those on law, religion, and manners.

These have a common underlying motive in an anxious questioning by the author of his seeming assumption that mind in Virginia is "ripening" into independence from its ancient relation to human nature. In his discussion of the making of the Virginia Constitution, Jefferson refers at some length to what he considers to have been the appalling desire by some members of the Assembly in 1776 to imitate the Roman practice of meeting an emergency by decreeing a dictatorship. Such a betrayal of freedom by fear, Jefferson says, was repugnant to any "who did not mean to expend his blood and substance for the wretched purpose of changing this master for that." Yet Jefferson intimates as *Notes on Virginia* proceeds that human nature may not be altogether subject to control of the rational will, and may harbor motives that lead it to prefer slavery over freedom. Referring to the failure of Virginians to separate church and state, he observes how people may will to give "their lives and fortunes for the establishment of civil freedom" and at the same time will to remain in "religious slavery." But Jefferson's doubt of the power of mind to become independent—to achieve the emancipation of human nature—is nowhere so graphically indicated as it is in his fear that, even if the Virginians are capable of freeing themselves from enslavement to both king and church, they may not be capable of freeing themselves from bondage to their own slaves. This fear emerges suddenly in the well-known apocalyptic vision of the fate of the slave masters in the eighteenth chapter of *Notes on Virginia*.

As he explains in the fourteenth chapter, Jefferson believed that sound scientific evidence showed that Africans
are an inferior race of the human species and thus not to be
assimilated by the superior white race without "staining"
its blood. Consequently, whereas in Rome—slaves there
being of the same color as the masters and frequently as well
educated—"emancipation required but one effort," in America a second effort, "unknown to history," is necessary: slaves
must be removed beyond the reach of mixture. Knowing as
he undoubtedly did that emancipation through colonization
could at best be never more than partial, Jefferson's fixation
on colonization as the sole rational solution to the problem
of slavery suggests that supporting colonization was at bot-
tom, and perhaps unconsciously, a way of rationalizing the
perpetuation of slavery. It is possible to interpret the apocalyptic vision of the fate of the slave masters in the eighteenth chapter of *Notes on Virginia* as a necessary release
from a tangle of reason and emotion that Jefferson was unable to contain within the bounds of his customary deco-
rum. In the same highly concentrated paragraph in which he
makes his entire response to Barbé-Marbois' query about
"customs and manners that happen to be received in that
state," Jefferson portrays the "whole commerce between
master and slave" as "a perpetual exercise of the most bois-
terous passions, the most unremitting despotism" on the
part of the masters, and makes the most eloquent and desperate appeal on behalf of "total emancipation" to be found
in the American literature of slavery. Only this, Jefferson
warns, will prevent the eventual "extirpation" of the moral
monsters who are the slave masters—this being accomplished either by the oppressed themselves or by "supernatural interference."[16]

In the era of the South's defense of slavery after his death,
Jefferson was anathematized as a traitor to his own community—a false witness from within the ranks of the slave-

16. *Ibid.*, 270, 288–89.

holders. He had misrepresented them, they felt, as much as the radical abolitionists, who made a profession of lying about life on the southern plantations. In view of the evidence about the actuality of plantation life at Mount Vernon, Sabine Hall, Montpelier, or Monticello, Jefferson did, to be sure, distort the observable fact of the everyday relationship of slaves and their masters; yet it would seem that, in doing so, he was like a poet or a novelist seeking through a symbolic fiction to represent the inner truth of his own historical time and place. Ten years before he began to work on *Notes on Virginia*, Jefferson devoted almost half the list of books he recommended for the library of young Robert Skipworth to novels, poems, and plays, arguing that these would serve to "fix" in his mind "the principles and practices of virtue"—these being "dispositions of the mind" that "acquire strength by exercise" of the moral feelings. "Considering history as a moral exercise," Jefferson wrote to Skipworth on August 3, 1771, "her lessons would be too infrequent if confined to real life." But in *Notes on Virginia* Jefferson abandoned the rational notion that the mind may be stimulated to exercise the "sympathetic emotion of Virtue" by a "fictitious" as well as by a "real personage." In a moment of Faulknerian intensity, he created a dark fiction of the plantation, in which he sees not only himself and his peers sunk in rage and indolence but envisions their children corrupted, probably beyond redemption, by "odious peculiarities" of character resulting from imitating their parents in the daily exercise of tyranny. At this moment, in the inward reaches of Jefferson's imagination, rational discrimination between "real life" and fiction vanished. Fiction and reality became twin aspects of history: history is consciousness and consciousness is history.

The most extraordinary aspect of the visionary treatment of slavery in the fervent moment of elevated consciousness in the eighteenth chapter of *Notes on Virginia* is Jefferson's according the slave a status he had never before granted him. Referring to the "statesman" who is guilty of "permitting one half the citizens . . . to trample on the rights of the other" and thus to destroy "the amor patriae of the other," Jefferson not only recognizes his African slave as a citizen—a political equal—but as an intellectual and moral equal. A momentary flash in *Notes on Virginia*, this recognition would not be repeated in Jefferson's voluminous writings, public or private.[17]

Notes on Virginia was begun a year after Virginia, while Jefferson was still in the governor's office, enacted legislation awarding soldiers engaged in the struggle for liberty three hundred acres of land and a slave. While this legislation assumed the supportive connection between republican liberty and slavery, Jefferson's book in its profound tensions is a deep questioning of this relation, reflecting a crisis in his whole sense of land, slaves, and mind. Declaring (in the eighteenth chapter) that total emancipation of the slaves is called for, Jefferson immediately confounds his own declaration by indicating that this may be impossible because the human mind, as represented by the slaveholder, is probably powerless—save by supernatural intervention—to emancipate itself from the historical situation of which it is an integral part. This suggestion—consonant with the representation of the mind of the slaveholder throughout *Notes on Virginia*—anticipates the description of the problematical identity of the master to be set forth twenty-five years later in Hegel's *Phenomenology of Mind* (1804). Since, Hegel observes, the identity of the master depends on the recognition he can win in a contest of wills with a consciousness he deems inferior to his own, the master can never enjoy the sense of an autonomous existence. But even though, in the dual role of slave master and man of letters, Jefferson fully lived the master-slave relationship that Hegel was to delineate—and in *Notes on Virginia* brought it almost to the level of explicit articulation—Jefferson refused finally to acknowledge the tensions and anxieties generated by his own experience of life in a so-

17. Jefferson to Robert Skipworth, August 3, 1771, in *Writings of Jefferson*, ed. Lipscomb and Bergh, IV, 239; *Notes on Virginia*, 288.

ciety based on slavery that yet aspired to incarnate a new ideal of freedom. Almost with his last words in 1826 he reaffirmed his lifelong conviction in the "free right to the unbounded exercise of reason and freedom and opinion." And he left instructions that as a testament to his conviction the monument marking his grave should record these three accomplishments: the authorship of the Declaration, the authorship of the statute for establishing religious freedom in Virginia, and the founding of the University of Virginia.

If any of these acts was potentially more important than the others, it was the final one. Although the process of the secularization of mind had originated in the later Middle Ages in the university—the major representation of the medieval ecumene of Latinity—this was also the place where the assimilation of mind to secular knowledge was most effectively resisted. Until the nineteenth and twentieth centuries, the third realm was more truly represented by institutions like the French Academy and the American Philosophical Society than by the university. The establishment of Jefferson's university, it may not be too much to say, was the first historical instance in which the university was conceived as being purely an agency of the secular realm of letters and learning.

Responding to the need to provide for the continuity of freedom in Virginia, and the nation—to the imperative to perpetuate the ideal of the "free right to the unbounded exercise of reason and opinion"—the University of Virginia, Jefferson envisaged, would institutionalize a new kind of relationship between the third realm and the state. It would educate an elite corps of young Virginians—the "intellectual aristocracy"—to be at one and the same time citizens of the American Republic and of the republic that is its originating and sustaining source, the republic of letters. To adapt a term employed by Jefferson's younger British contemporary, Samuel Taylor Coleridge, in his study entitled *On the Constitution of Church and State According to the Idea of*

Each (1830), the Jeffersonian educated elite would constitute
a wholly secular version of the class Coleridge calls the "clerisy." The graduates of "Mr. Jefferson's University" would be
an American clerisy—the inheritors of the intellectual patriciate that had made the Revolution and in substantial part
invented the nation.

That in actual history the post-Jeffersonian southern intellectuals constituted a sectional clerisy of proslavery idea-
logues does not, contrary to some opinion, indicate that they
were less than the direct inheritors of the Jeffersonian dream
of an intellectual aristocracy. The passage from the Jeffersonian to the post-Jeffersonian culture of mind in the South
was strongly coherent in that it was a continuation of the
Jeffersonian subscription to the great critique of tradition;
only in the superficial sense was the post-Jeffersonian mind
in the South a reactionary effort to recover past structures of
order. Accepting the equation of land, slaves, and mind in a
more literal, less questioning way than had Jefferson, his inheritors effected the ultimate suppression of the irony of
slavery in their central doctrine. Stated by the Virginia philosopher of history, Thomas Roderick Dew, this held that
the institution of chattel slavery is the "sheet anchor" of
American liberty.[18]

This doctrine was, in the opinion of many southerners, ab-
solutely supported by the rational interpretation of the disposition of federal and state powers under the Constitution,
the right both to own and to sell slaves being inherent in the
wisdom of the order decreed by the Constitution. Even when
the social theorists of the southern clerisy—under the increasing pressure of the Protestant evangelical movement—
began to seek justification for what the rationalist Henry
Hughes in his *Treatise on Sociology: Theoretical and Practical* (1854) termed "the societary organization of the United
States South" in a greater authority than that of the human

18. Thomas Roderick Dew, "Republicanism and Literature," in Michael
O'Brien (ed.), *All Clever Men Who Make Their Way: Critical Discourse in
the Old South* (Fayetteville, Ark., 1982), 170.

mind, they did not reverse the context of southern history—
that is, the modern movement of history into mind.[19] The
southern intellectuals turned over the rationalistic coin of
the Enlightenment ethos, and instead of continuing to secu-
larize the spiritual, so to speak, spiritualized the secular.
As time went on, southern high culture tended to become
heavily associated with evangelical Protestantism. Proslavery advocates accepted a theology based on the literal interpretation of the Bible—a book they read in the tense of the
historical present—and, analyzing the language and content
of the Bible, decoded its revelation of their own meaning in
history. Southern theologians, as Eugene Genovese and Elizabeth Fox-Genovese are currently demonstrating in their brilliant inquiries into the Old South as a religious society,
could on the basis of literal biblical evidence out-argue any-
body who claimed biblical sanction for abolition. But the
partnership of the secular theorists and the theologians was
not altogether, maybe not even primarily, inspired by the requirements of the defense of slavery. It was a union, Genovese and Fox-Genovese observe, in which the "high culture"
of the southern intellectuals linked itself intimately to—became the shaping force of—"the *mentalité*—the daily be-
liefs and practices of both slaveholding and nonslaveholding
southerners," thereby providing them with a "coherent
world view" and imparting to "southern culture, for all its
regional, racial, and class variants," a sense of hierarchical
community, at once cohesive and historically unique.[20]

With ironic consistency, the radical southern reactionary
George Fitzhugh could say, on the one hand, "We want no

19. Henry Hughes, *Treatise on Sociology*, as excerpted in *The Ideology
of Slavery: Proslavery Thought in the Old South, 1830–1860*, ed. Drew
Gilpin Faust (Baton Rouge, 1983), 241.
20. See Eugene Genovese and Elizabeth Fox-Genovese, "The Religious
Ideals of Southern Slave Society," *Georgia Historical Quarterly*, LXX
(Spring, 1986), 1–16. See also Eugene D. Genovese, *The World the Slaveholders Made: Two Essays in Interpretation* (1969; rpr. Middletown, Conn.,
1988), especially the introduction (pp. iv–xxii) by Genovese to this new
Wesleyan University Press edition.

new world," and proclaim, on the other hand, on the eve of
the Civil War, "We alone are a new people."[21] Grounded in
their secular-spiritual "societary organization," southerners
followed William Harper in his noted essay "Slavery in the
Light of Social Ethics" in proclaiming slavery as the "sole
cause" of civilization. Moving toward the innovative development of an imperialistic modern nation-state, some of the
more exuberant southern dreamers conceived a southern nation that would extend its culture of land, mind, and slaves
not only across the American West but, making the Gulf of
Mexico into the South's Mediterranean Sea, embrace a dominion that would include the Caribbean islands, Central
America, and maybe most of South America. In their attempt to transform their society into a novel nation-state,
the southerners failed. In this failure, particularly in the
emancipation of the slaves that resulted, we herald a victory
for freedom; but, as we know, it was no simple, definitive
victory. For one thing, the emancipation of the slaves from
the burden of chattel slavery did not emancipate the nation
from the burden of slavery in other forms, including the economic and social reenslavement of the former chattels.

But I shall at this point turn more in the direction of another historical irony to observe that the failure of antebellum southern society was also the failure of antebellum
New England society. With the failure of these societies, the
Republic that Jefferson and Adams played so large a part in
inventing and establishing in history became the lost cause
not only of the South, which seceded from the Union in
order to be true to its vision of this Republic, but of New England, which committed itself to the Union in order to be
true to its vision of the Republic of Jefferson and Adams. The
irreconcilable tension between these opposing salvational
efforts doomed the first American Republic.

21. George Fitzhugh, "German Literature," *DeBow's Review*, XXVII
(September, 1860), 289. I am indebted to Professor Fred Hobson for this
reference.

II Slavery and the Cultural Imperialism of New England

I remember a late summer afternoon in a pleasant lecture room at a well-known New England college, where several years ago at the invitation of the English faculty I went to give a couple of lectures. After speaking informally in the morning to a large group of undergraduates on the fate of Quentin Compson in Faulkner's *The Sound and the Fury* and responding to questions from some of the students, I realized once again that the southerner in New England may even yet be regarded either as a historical curiosity or, more compassionately, a cultural exotic. The afternoon lecture, a formal essay on the subject of southern literature and slavery, was presented before an audience composed largely of faculty, with only a sprinkling of students in attendance. Since the obligatory faculty party for the off-campus speaker was scheduled shortly after the lecture, no period had been reserved for questions following my presentation. But after I finished reading, four or five persons momentarily circled around the lectern. While talking with them I noticed an attractive blonde-haired girl on the periphery of the group; obviously an undergraduate, she seemed to be waiting until she had the chance to speak to me privately. As the little group broke up and I was restoring the lecture manuscript to my briefcase, she moved closer and said quietly, "You know, I feel awfully guilty about slavery."

I was a little taken back and replied awkwardly, as I recall, with the usual attempt at professorial paternalism, "Is that so? Where are you from?" She said, "Massachusetts." I remember I started to say, "Well, that figures." But I didn't. In fact, I guess I failed to say much of anything. I did not even

33

ask her name. But I hardly needed to learn this. Her speech, manner, and general bearing made her New England background plain; and in any event she did not pause for further preliminaries before getting on with what she had to say. This was brief, but somehow it seemed to involve me in the triple role of professor, confessor, and sinner; for, if I heard her correctly, she was, as students will do at times, at once telling me about her own emotional state and in some measure making me—an elderly white southern professor (elderly by her sense of time at least)—responsible for the pain she felt. In the aftermath of my pretty auditor's strangely accusatorial little confession, I believe I made some lame academic comments about the complexity of ethnic guilt in American culture. But she had made her statement and was, I realized, not inclined to say more, and I was delaying my host for the social occasion. We walked out of the room and parted in the hall with a pleasantry or two; and I went on to the party, where nobody even mentioned slavery. Yet I had an uncertain but vaguely uncomfortable feeling even in that congenial company that I might have crossed an indeterminate border and come into another country.

I told myself later that the Massachusetts maid was hardly sophisticated enough to have had any very deliberate intent in speaking her mind, but I could not escape the feeling that somehow, as the belated inheritor of a lost New England, she had felt compelled to reprove a lost South; and that I, as a descendant of the lost South, had been compelled, even against my moral convictions about slavery, somehow to resent it. I told myself too that in involving ourselves in an old antagonism the young lady and I were cultural anachronisms. The war was over.

Or is it? In view of the fact that as I move along in these remarks I will be placing an emphasis on the opposition between Virginia and Massachusetts, the story of my small New England encounter would work better if I were from Virginia instead of Texas and Louisiana. Yet the little tale is relevant to a stress I want to put on the antebellum relationship between New England and the South that, I venture to say, has not been so much neglected as suppressed in the study of American history.

I refer to the question of New England nationalism. We have devoted a great deal of time to exploring the subject of the development of American nationalism, and we have spent almost as much time investigating the subject of southern nationalism. But we have by and large assumed that after an ineffective gesture toward secession led by a small group from Essex County, Massachusetts, in 1814–15—among them Timothy Pickering and others of the educated elite in the state—the New England intellect increasingly associated itself with the image of the Union. The classic instance is that of New England's most famous intellectual, Ralph Waldo Emerson, who in describing the character of the "American Scholar" to the Harvard Phi Beta Kappa Society in 1837 had, as James Russell Lowell said, set forth the declaration of American literary and cultural independence. Yet in the distinction that the New England intellectuals made between the culture of mind in New England and the culture of mind (or lack of it) in the South we scarcely discover the sentiment of a cohesive American nationalism. Emerson was alienated for years from the Union because it included the southern states. He became a Unionist only with the coming of the Civil War, when it seemed to him that through the Union it might be possible to destroy the South and to imprint the American nation with the indelible stamp of New England culture.

Obviously in the case of Emerson I speak of a more volatile New Englandism than that represented by George Ticknor. As I indicated earlier, the culture of mind in the South and in New England tended to be based on mutually exclusive assumptions: that the South represented the truth of the Republic; that New England represented the truth of the Republic. In this situation, even cosmopolitans like Ticknor and Jefferson were paradoxically obedient respectively to New Englandism and Southernism. But there was a greater paradox in the situation, and this was the way New England intellectuals like Emerson shaped American cultural nationalism even as they were in a state of virtual secession from the American Union. I will shortly come directly to Emerson. But first let me take up more fully than I have done so far certain historical aspects of the high culture of the South and the high culture of New England.

To begin with, it is of some significance to recall—as curiously enough indigenous historians of New England seldom seem to do—that at the beginning of the English settlement of the Atlantic seaboard the territory to become known as New England was under the supervision of the North Virginia Company and was known as North Virginia; the territory of South Virginia, almost from the first called simply Virginia, was under the charge of the South Virginia Company. Although fate decreed that Captain John Smith was not to return to colonize the northern territory, as he ardently aspired to do, this adventurer, explorer, and colonizer considered himself to be not only the chief figure in the Jamestown settlement, but in the Plymouth and Massachusetts Bay settlements as well. In testimony to his association with the initial colonizing of New England, Smith could point both to his crucial exploring and mapping activities along the northern Atlantic seaboard in 1614 and to the fact that he himself (thinking of the name "Nouvelle France") had renamed the land of North Virginia and called it New England. Then, too, he could cite the magisterial title conferred on him after his return from the 1614 voyage: Admiral of New England. Although the legitimacy of this title may be questioned (Smith may have conferred it on himself), it was an appropriate recognition of the seminal role he had played and was yet to play in the history of New England (and surely it was a proper recognition of his importance as a seafarer).

Then, too, the title added authority not only to Smith as an actor in the drama of colonization but, more significantly, to

Smith as the author of the historical drama of the South and North Virginias. I refer especially to Smith's promotional tract entitled *A Description of New England: or the Observations, and Discovieries, of Captain John Smith (Admirall of That Country) in the North of America, in the Year of Our Lord 1614,* and to another tract, written six years before, entitled *A True Relation of Such Occurrences and Accidents of Noate as Hath Happened in Virginia Since the First Planting of the Collony, Which Is Now Resident in the South Part Thereof, till the Last Returne from Thence.* In 1624 Smith, by this time author of five or six books dealing with colonizing efforts on the Atlantic seaboard, unified his story of the two Virginias in *The Generall Historie of Virginia, New-England, and the Summer Isles.* Although the ascription of authorship on the title page of *A True Relation* reads merely "By Captaine John Smith, one of the said collony," Smith could have rightfully referred to himself as "president" or "governor" of South Virginia. Later on, he was less modest. When in 1624 he brought together all of his writings to date about the colonization endeavor, Smith enhanced the facts and ascribed the authorship of *The Generall Historie of Virginia, New-England, and the Summer Isles* to "Captaine John Smith, sometimes governor of those countryes & Admirall of New England."

Although this exaggerated claim—Smith was never governor of New England or Bermuda—may be regarded simply as evidence that Smith was something of a braggart (or, as some have said, a pathological liar), his proprietary attitude toward the New World settlements was an aspect of his endeavor to compensate for his frustrated desire for wealth, fame, and power. As he grew older, finding himself not only wifeless and childless (possibly because he had been rendered impotent in an accidental gunpowder explosion while he was at Jamestown) but devoid of any family association, Smith fancifully conceived of the new colonies as his manorial estate. Employing the license of the Elizabethan conceit, he wrote in the *Generall Historie:* "By that acquaintance I

have with them [Virginia and New England], I call them my
children; for they have beene my Wife, my Hawks, Hounds,
my Cards, my Dice, and in totall my best content, as indif-
ferent to my heart, as my left hand to my right. And not-
withstanding, all those miracles of disasters have crossed
both them and me, yet were there not an Englishman re-
maining . . . I would yet begin againe with as small meanes
as I did at first."[1]

By the time Smith created this metaphorical expression of
his relation to Virginia and New England, he had failed in
three attempts to get back to New England and had no tangible stake in either. Getting on in years and without a sufficient income, he was more or less dependent, it would seem,
on the financial assistance of friends to keep body and soul
together. But although he had no part in it and would never
even see the first actual settlement in New England at Plymouth in 1620, Smith describes it in the last chapter of the
Generall Historie as though he knew it at first hand (though
he knew about it mostly from *Mourt's Relation* of 1622).
Here he also speaks of the "Virgins Sister, now called New
England, at my humble sute" as the justification of his own
endeavors to plant this other part of Virginia with Englishmen. At the end of his life, writing his final testament to his
career as colonizer, *Advertisements for the Unexperienced
Planters of New England, or Any Where, or, the Path-way to
Experience to Erect a Plantation* (1631), Smith expanded the
story of the colonization of the "Virgins sister" by a brief description of the second, and most portentous, New England
settlement, that of the Puritans in the Massachusetts Bay
area in 1629. At the same time he expanded his metaphorical relationship to Virginia and New England, saying that he
still hoped to live out the rest of his life in America and to
make his children, Virginia and New England, "my heires,
executors, administrators and assignes."

Smith was aware at this point, of course, that there was no

1. *The Complete Works of Captain John Smith, 1580–1631*, ed. Philip L.
Barbour (3 vols.; Chapel Hill, 1986), II, 462.

possibility of his returning to America and of the obvious fact that he had neither tangible property nor money to assign to anyone. But, as the title of his last book states, he did have advice, both practical and prophetic, to bequeath to his "children." None he offered was more prescient, and, it may be said, more redolent of the pathos of history, than that contained in the prophetic qualification of his hope that the people of the older colony would be helpful and comforting to their new neighbors in New England. "But I feare," Smith adds,

> the seed of envy, and the rust of covetousnesse doth grow too fast, for some would have all men advance Virginia to the ruine of New-England; and others the losse of Virginia to sustaine New-England, which God in his mercy forbid; for at first it was intended by that most memorable Judge Sir John Popham, then Lord chiefe Justice of England, and the Lords of his Majesties Privy Councel, with divers others, that two Colonies should be planted, as now they be, for the better strengthening each other against all occurrences; the which to performe, shal ever be in my hearty prayers to Almighty God, and to increase and continue that mutuall love betwixt them for ever.[2]

The aura of tragic irony that hovers about Smith's premonition of an inevitable antagonism between Virginia and New England is no doubt cast by our own historical hindsight, especially by our recognition on the far side of Appomattox of how limited Smith was in his comprehension of the intensive and complex motives of the dissenters who came to Massachusetts. Aware only that they threatened to present the problem of, as he says in the *Advertisements*, "the miserable effects of faction in Religion," he naïvely admonishes those who had gone to all the trouble to place a forbidding ocean between themselves and the English establishment to abide yet by the "prime authority" they had so strenuously rejected as the sole source of a "well setled Common-wealth."[3]

2. *Ibid.*, III, 300, 274–75.
3. *Ibid.*, III, 296–97.

Yet Smith bequeathed to his children, Virginia and New England, more than such nostalgic counsel. In *A True Relation* and his other books he left the first recording of the effort to realize intellectually, so to speak, the possibilities of an organized settlement of the American wilderness by literate, enterprising Jacobeans. An effort that involved the use of force as an expediency rather than as policy, it depended for its success on the use of the kind of mind Lionel Trilling has described as coming into being in the fifteenth century, the mind that would be the source and model of modern forms of societal and political order: a mind invested with energy, intentionality, the power of discerning relations, and the capacity for looking both forward and backward. In a limited but distinct way, this is the mind we see at work in *A True Relation* and even more so in Smith's subsequent books about the Atlantic settlement.

But Smith did not have an entire confidence in the power of intelligence. Although he was quite cognizant of the fact that he lived in the age of the mechanical clock, the mariner's compass, the telescope, and the printing press—in the age, in short, of his compatriot in the Virginia Company, Sir Francis Bacon—and thus was aware, if not explicitly so, of the Virginia settlement as a response to the movement of history into mind, Smith still owed a strong allegiance to the society of king and altar. His sense of the old society as the proper model of the colonial society tended to block any realization on his part that he was actually the prophet of, and even a participant in, the modern reversal of society and mind. Yet Smith shared in the Elizabethan and Jacobean prescience of change, notably so in the foreboding tension we discern in his works between his hope for the future relationship of Virginia and New England (or Massachusetts) and his strained and awkward attempt to bring these colonies into the self-conceived embrace of his patriarchal concern and love and thus to imagine them to be in a state of familial love. Smith, like Sir Robert Filmer in *Patriarcha*, intellectualized traditional order. In doing so, he implicitly prophesied that Virginia and Massachusetts were destined to bring the power of ideas to bear upon the nature of society in such a way that each would seek to destroy the other.

If Smith could have returned in another ten years or so to visit the Virginia colony he had helped to establish and the Massachusetts colony he had helped to prepare the way for but had never seen, he might have had an intimation that the antagonism that he had prophesied would rise between the "Virgin and the Virgins sister" would be more complex than he had envisioned. This would have been notably so if he had heard the interpretation of history offered from the pulpits of Massachusetts and in the printed works of the chief authors and actors in the New England drama, the New England intellectuals—the learned ministry—as the Cromwellian rebellion and the civil wars developed in Old England. To be sure, Smith might have had considerable difficulty comprehending what was being said, the literature of the New England planting being so markedly different from that of the Virginia planting. For instance, he would have failed to find anyone in New England appealing to a familial image of the relationship between the southern and the northern colonies; for, although the little band of Pilgrims had, with the assistance of Sir Edwin Sandys, secured permission to take up land in the domain of the London (or Virginia) Company, they had made their landfall at Cape Cod, outside the jurisdiction of their sponsor, and had no further connection with the Virginia enterprise (though we must always wonder what would have happened had the Pilgrims been able to stay on course). The Massachusetts Bay Colony had come into existence under a royal charter after the dissolution of the London Company.

Yet, aware of what was to happen between Virginia and Massachusetts, we cannot but be fascinated by certain intimations of the future that, assuming a broad poetic license, we may read into the writings of the first generation or two of New England's own prophetic visionaries. This may be

particularly so if we do what the Puritans never did and employ the Puritan prophetic technique of "typology" to link
events in secular rather than in biblical history. I am thinking about one instance in the early New England reaction to
the outbreak of the great civil conflict in their homeland, a
sermon entitled "New England's Tears for Old England's
Fears" preached in Boston by the Reverend William Hooke
on a day of fasting and humiliation proclaimed for New England on July 23, 1640, as a response to the news of the
crisis.

Contrary to what we may expect, Hooke's sermon is neither a rallying cry for support of the rebellion nor a castiga-
tion of monarchy and church. As Alan Heimert and Andrew
Delbanco observe in *The Puritans in America,* Hooke trans-
forms the day of humiliation into "something of a day of
thanksgiving, even of congratulation," for "the refuge" the
New England Puritans enjoy "from the death and desola-
tion" in Old England. In developing his sermonic mood
Hooke draws on all his rhetorical power to describe the
awfulness of war in general and of civil war in particular. In-
voking the full horror of the developing conflict in England,
he rather strangely and somewhat ambiguously depicts a
struggle not simply between two factions within the nation
but between two "nations" within the nation: "And not to
look upon the occasions given on the one side or the other,
between the two sister nations (sister nations? ah, the word
woundeth), let us look this day simply on the event, a sad
event in all likelihood, the dividing of a king from his sub-
jects, and him from them, their mutual taking up of arms in
opposition and defense; the consequences, even the gloomy
and dark consequence thereof, are killing and slaying, and
sacking and burning, and robbing, and rifyling, cursing and
blaspheming, &c." There are "no wars," Hooke exclaims,
"so unnatural, so desolating, as civil wars. You have heard,
Beloved, of the dreadful German wars; why if there are any
in our own country this day, I may call them German wars,

because they are the wars of Germans, even the bloody contentions of brethren; and when relations turn opposites, nothing more opposite. A kingdom at wars with a foreign enemy may stand, but a kingdom divided against itself, can never."[4] One can hardly read Hooke's sermon today without feeling that it embodied an eerie prophecy of what was to come. "The Virgin" and "the Virgins sister" would jointly lead a sanguinary revolution against a king; in what at times would be civil war among themselves the colonists would commit a symbolic regicide; they would thereafter cooperate in constructing an American republic, compromising differences and even acting at times as though they were of common mind, only in a few decades to become engaged in a non-negotiable and desperate conflict about what each represented in history.

The once popular historical fantasy that this bloody drama of representation centered in an opposition between Southern Cavaliers and New England Puritans—that is to say, that it was somehow a replication of the seventeenth-century encounter between the Royalists and the Roundheads—may even today distort our image of the character of the opponents in the American Civil War. But if so, this is not so much because we still ignore the complexity of the southern motive to achieve independent representation in history; it is because we fail to recognize that even at the time of the Civil War New England responded to a desire to assert itself as a historical entity as old as the first generation of New Englanders, when, so to speak, the Puritan migrants became transfigured Roundheads. In their compulsion to leave their homeland for a New Canaan, Heimert and Delbanco observe, the Puritans were moved not by "an ideology" or a "coherent critique of the standing church" but by an extreme "emotion of dissent." Transplanted to a place where the enemies of the migrants "seemed weak and far away,"

4. Alan Heimert and Andrew Delbanco (eds.), *The Puritans in America: A Narrative Anthology* (Cambridge, Mass., 1985), 103, 105.

their emotion underwent a "complex adjustment to being unopposed." The result was that in America the Puritans "turned inward with merciless demands on the self that can make their English brethren seem lenient," and they were soon "rooting out deviants" in the community. "The irony of this transformation from dissenters to lawgivers," Heimert and Delbanco observe, "is manifold and deep; with it comes a certain queasiness in the Puritan voice as it tries to find its American pitch."[5] Perhaps the Heimert-Delbanco interpretation may be put in still more forceful terms: the New England migrants who had left home for good—and the majority of them elected not to return to take part in the conflict in the old home—tacitly effected a secession from the Puritan nation of dissenters within a nation that had developed in Old England, and in doing so had come to represent not the transplanted offspring of a parent nation but a people engaged—however uncertainly and anxiously—in defining not the "Old England Way" but a "New England Way," and thus in effect becoming a new nation.

This perception was first clearly voiced by the founder of Concord, Massachusetts—a direct ancestor of Ralph Waldo Emerson—the Reverend Peter Bulkeley, who in the second edition of *The Gospel-Covenant* (1651) offered a famous admonishment to the New England nation that it was uniquely bound to, if I may phrase it thus, a world-historical covenant with God.

> And as for ourselves here, the people of New England, we should in a special manner labor to shine forth in holiness above other people; we have that plenty and abundance of ordinances and means of grace, as few people enjoy the like. We are as a city set upon an hill, in the open view of all the earth; the eyes of the world are upon us because we profess ourselves to be a people in covenant with God, and therefore not only the Lord our God, with whom we have made covenant, but heaven and earth, angels and men, that are witnesses to our profession, will cry

5. *Ibid.*, 15.

shame upon us, if we walk contrary to the covenant which we have professed and promised to walk in. If we open the mouths of men against our profession by reason of the scandal of our lives, we (of all men) shall have the greater sin.

. . . let us study so to walk, that this may be our excellency and dignity among the nations of the world, among which we live: That they may be constrained to say of us, "Only this people is wise, an holy and blessed people," that all that see us may see and know that the name of the Lord is called upon us, and that we are the seed which the Lord hath blessed, Deuteronomy 28:10, Isaiah 61:9. There is no people but will strive to excel in some thing; what can we excel in, if not in holiness?[6]

Peter Bulkeley's vision anticipates the growth of the millenarian conviction in the last half of the seventeenth century, when some New Englanders would locate the New Jerusalem, the great terminal city in human history before the end of the world, in New England. Although a decided secularization of its seventeenth-century cultural heritage is evident in the growth of commerce and the liberalization of religion in New England during the eighteenth century, this was relative to the persistence of a strong emotional attachment to the idea, or ideal, of New Englanders as a select people, a particular group of Puritans chosen by God to constitute, as Peter Bulkeley had proclaimed, a nation "among the nations of the world." In what Emerson called "the interior and spiritual history of New England," the publication within a two-year span of Benjamin Franklin's *Proposal for Promoting Useful Knowledge Among the British Plantations of America* (1743) and Jonathan Edwards' *Some Thoughts Concerning the Present Revival of Religion in New England* (1742) is not a coincidence.

In the first work, Franklin essentially announces the world-historical intention of modern secular mind to bring under its dominion "a long tract" of continental wilderness stretching "from Nova Scotia to Georgia" and "extending

6. *Ibid.*, 120.

North and South thro' different climates, having different soils, producing different plants, mines and minerals, and capable of different improvements, manufactures, &c."[7] Before moving to Philadelphia to become America's greatest bourgeois intellectual, the author of the *Proposal for Promoting Useful Knowledge* had in his native Boston served a crucial apprenticeship in the printing trade, and a still more crucial self-directed apprenticeship to writing. Far more than being the mere background of his life, Franklin's experience of New England is the key to his major significance: namely, a secularization of the New England Way—at times a blatant, at times a subtle process that is implicit in his life and thought from his authorship of the "Silence Dogood" essays in the *New England Courant* in the early 1720s to his role in the American Revolution and the making of the United States Constitution.

The work by Edwards—born in Connecticut and educated at the College of New Haven (later to become Yale University), and subsequently for many years minister in his grandfather Solomon Stoddard's old parish in Northampton, Massachusetts—is an announcement of a new awakening to the meaning of the Puritan exodus from England into the American wilderness. Although Edwards carefully avoided subscribing to New England provinciality, he did not fail to consider that the "circumstances of the settlement of New England" made it "appear the most likely" place in the American colonies for the "glorious work" toward the millennial future to "take its rise." Edwards was in effect renewing and expanding a spiritual heritage that demanded a vision of New England's world-historical covenant with the Calvinistic God, which promised to make New England the symbol and substance of the truth of the biblical revelation of the millenarian fulfillment of history.

Yet in his attachment to the renewal of the New England mission Edwards—like Franklin, in his own way a represen-

7. *Ibid.*, 406.

tative genius of the age—was quite aware that he must turn not only to the construction of a new image of the natural world and its possibilities but to the construction of a new image of the processes of mind itself and the accommodation of this image to the Calvinistic world view. In his *Treatise on the Religious Affections* (1745), Edwards abandoned the old "faculty psychology" and embraced the new psychology associated with Locke. Earlier, in *Justification by Faith*, he had argued that the Newtonian discovery of gravity had disclosed a new metaphor for divine and human love. Employing a sophisticated grasp of metaphor—I am relying once more on Heimert and Delbanco—Edwards tended to justify the emotional structure of faith by an analytical procedure, and thus to create a deep tension between spiritual and intellectual perception. Although his career flowered well past the theocratic moment in New England history, it was yet the most forceful embodiment of the exhilarating New England equation of piety, intellect, and the sense of belonging, like the Israelites, to a chosen nation.[8]

Had Edwards had the support of the intellectual capital of New England, we may well suppose that the history of New England, and perhaps that of the country as a whole, might be different. But by the time Edwards was at his height, Boston was, from the Calvinistic point of view, showing signs of becoming a seat of heresy. At the very beginning of the eighteenth century Benjamin Colman had introduced instrumental music into the services at the Brattle Street Church, and by the time of the Revolution the liberal opinions of Charles Chauncy and others were commonplace in Boston. When the appointment of a known liberal to the chair of theology at Harvard in 1805 led to the outbreak of an open controversy between the liberals and the Calvinists—who by then were mostly outside the city—it at times caused great bitterness, but the fight was largely anachronistic. The Bostonians, whether they wanted to pin on the

8. See *ibid.*, 409–13.

label of Unitarian or not, had ceased to be Trinitarians. As has been often pointed out, they had moved from a pietistic to a moralistic faith.

Yet although the Bostonians accepted Unitarian principles as the proper Boston Way and, as far as they were concerned, the proper New England Way—which promoted a still greater Boston insularity than had before existed—the historic image of New England as the homeland of God's chosen prophets and lawgivers continued to be a powerful recurrent element of the poetry of New England culture. It remained so until its final expression in the career of Emerson, who, in spite of the fact that his forebears would have condemned him as the grossest of heretics and hounded him out of the land or worse, fulfilled the poetry of the Puritan culture. In view of his effort to renew once more the imperial equation of spirit, intellect, and New England nationhood, in fact he may be called the last of the line of Puritan prophetic intellectuals, or of Puritan "prophet-intellectuals." Beginning with Thomas Hooker, John Cotton, and Samuel Shepherd, this line descends to Cotton Mather and Jonathan Edwards, and finally, after a long hiatus, to Emerson.

Moving from the background of New England cultural imperialism in the seventeenth and eighteenth centuries to its foreground in the nineteenth century, I single out Emerson, I realize, somewhat arbitrarily, and save for the necessity of economy I would not do so. But in obeying necessity I choose to concentrate on Emerson because, for one thing, he was not only the leading New England intellectual in the antebellum age but by the 1850s he was recognized by many Americans, including some southerners, as the leading American intellectual. For another thing, he was internationally recognized as a significant American thinker and writer. Another reason I have in mind for concentrating on Emerson—a more subtle reason but the most important one—is that, like Jefferson, Emerson was a radical, expansive thinker. Often assumed, like Jefferson, to be a singular representation of mind in America—indeed, to be a singular representation of the *American* mind, the "representative" American intellectual—Emerson, like Jefferson, subscribed to the cosmopolitan autonomy of mind; yet, like Jefferson, he was ultimately obedient to the inner imperatives imposed on his representation of mind by his historical relation to his native state.

But the situation is more complex in the instance of Emerson than of Jefferson. Being a "transcendentalist" who believed that the human mind could through it own capacities transcend its inherence in human history, Emerson, unlike Jefferson, followed a kind of dialectical mode of thinking. As F. O. Matthiessen says, Emerson inveterately stated "things in opposites."[9] Proclaiming in one of his proverbial dicta that "a foolish consistency is the hobgoblin of little minds," he did not fear contradicting himself, since one could not contradict truth, its source being in the self's ultimate power of intuitive perception. Yet one of the curiosities of his thought is that—although the dialectical mode is evident in his journals as he struggled with such problems as the slavery question, the character of the Negro, secession and unionism, and the moral character of New England—Emerson carries on no debate with himself about the character of the world below the Mason-Dixon line. His attitude was virtually always negative and denunciatory. Without any specific anticipation in earlier journals, it abruptly appears in full-blown form in a journal entry for October, 1837. If the date affixed to the entry is correct—and it appears to be—this passage was set down about a month after Emerson had challenged the scholars of the Harvard Phi Beta Kappa chapter to redeem the culture of mind in America from its bondage to Europe. Let me present the entry in its entirety:

> The young Southerner comes here a spoiled child with graceful manners, excellent self command, very good to be spoiled more, but good for nothing else, a mere parader. He has con-

9. F. O. Matthiessen, *American Renaissance: Art and Expression in the Age of Emerson and Whitman* (New York, 1941), 3.

versed so much with rifles, horses, & dogs that he is become himself a rifle, a horse, & a dog and in civil educated company where anything human is going forward he is dumb & unhappy; like an Indian in a church. Treat them with great deference as we often do, and they accept it all as their due without misgiving. Give them an inch & they take a mile. They are mere bladders of conceit. Each snippersnapper of them all undertakes to speak for the entire Southern states. "At the South, the reputation of Cambridge" &c. &c. which being interpreted, is, In my negro village of Tuscaloosa or Cheraw or St Marks I supposed so & so. "We, at the South," forsooth. They are more civilized than the Seminoles, however, in my opinion; a little more. Their question respecting any man is like a Seminole's, How can he fight? In this country, we ask, What can he do? His pugnacity is all they prize, in man, dog, or turkey. The proper way of treating them is not deference but to say as Mr Ripley does "Fiddle faddle" in answer to each solemn remark about "The South." "It must be confessed" said the young man, "that in Alabama, we are dead to every thing, except as respects politics." "Very true," replied Mr Ripley, "leaving out the last clause." [10]

I do not know whether or not there were any students from the South among the Phi Beta Kappas who heard Emerson's adjuration that they each one become "Man Thinking." If there were, I doubt that Emerson cared; I doubt too that he cared about the fact, which he must have known, that the parent chapter of Phi Beta Kappa had been instituted by undergraduates at William and Mary in Williamsburg, Virginia, in 1776, to be followed two years later by a chapter at Yale and five years later by the Harvard chapter. Indeed, it seems clear that in his description of southern students Emerson had discovered an absolute cultural contrast between the South and New England: the one was a culture of no mind, the other a culture of mind.

How Emerson made this discovery is not at all clear, since no entries in his journals preceding the one about southern

10. *The Journals and Miscellaneous Notebooks of Ralph Waldo Emerson*, ed. William H. Gilman *et al.* (16 vols.; Cambridge, Mass., 1960–82), V, 388–89.

boys at Harvard show that he had been debating either with himself or with others about the character of the South; few earlier passages even mention the South or southerners, save those before 1837 recording the rather sparse account of a journey to South Carolina and Florida that Emerson, then a young minister, took during the first two or three months of 1827. Seeking relief from a threatening lung condition, he traveled by boat to Charleston but, finding the weather there unfavorable, went on to St. Augustine for several weeks. (His having been in Florida is presumably the reason he compares southerners to Seminoles in the satirical outburst I quoted above.) After his health improved, Emerson returned to Boston via Charleston. Devoting himself mostly to religious themes, he wrote little in his journals during the period of the southward journey about his reaction either to Charleston or St. Augustine. He mentions with approval the social graces of Charlestonians; even the slaves he saw on the streets, he says, observed the proprieties of cordial exchange. "Indeed," he says, "I have never seen an awkward Carolinian." In St. Augustine he set down a brief account of his attendance at a meeting of a Bible society in a building adjacent to a yard in which a slave auction was in progress. "One ear," Emerson remarks, "therefore heard the glad tidings of great joy whilst the other was regaled with 'Going gentlemen, Going!' And almost without changing our position we might aid in sending the scriptures into Africa or bid for 'four children without the mother' who had been kidnapped therefrom." The tone in which the little story is told is mildly ironic. But Emerson plainly regarded the conjunction of the religious meeting and the slave auction as being of more exotic than moral interest; he paralleled it with an anecdote about a Methodist preacher who denounced the president of the Bible society for his habitual cursing. The truth is that, while Emerson always regarded slavery unfavorably and by 1835 was praying to God that he would "never incur the disgrace of articulating one word of apology for the slave trader or slave-holder," his sensitivity either to slavery as an American institution or to the condition of the enslaved in America was at the time of his first notable writing—*Nature,* "The American Scholar," "The Divinity School Address"— still largely rhetorical.[11]

If Emerson's association between the evil of slavery and life in the South does not account for his attitude toward the southern boys at Harvard—or in the more general sense, for his summary relegation of half the United States to a condition of unredeemable barbarism—we may well wonder what the rationale of the comment he wrote in 1837 may truly be. One possibility is, of course, that Emerson was progressively caught up in the growing fashion in certain northern quarters of South-hating; clearly his portrayal of the southern boys as products of a mindless culture anticipates his later overt attacks on the South as a mindless slave society. But the underlying rationale of Emerson's hostile attitude toward southern society—its originating and dominant motive—is to be found in his attachment to the imperial idea of New England culture. We see this motive—do we not?—in "The American Scholar," which reflects not so much Emerson's will to become the spokesman of an American mind in process of formation as his effort to imagine himself as a New England intellectual engaged in assimilating the mind of the new Republic to the culture of mind in New England. Yet this effort of the imagination, for all its seeming expansive breadth, ruled out—as we see in the harsh criticism of southerners at Harvard—the possibility of assimilating the South to the New England mind.

One reason for Emerson's antipathy to the South unquestionably was his subscription to a sense of alienation between New England and the South that had its most immediate roots in an arch antipathy of the New England Federalists toward southern culture. Fisher Ames, a leading

11. *Ibid.,* III, 59, 117, V, 15.

spokesman for this attitude, summed it up when Jefferson became the third president of the United States: "New England now contains a million and half of inhabitants, of all colonies that ever were founded, the largest, the most assimilated, and to use the modern jargon, nationalized, the most respectable and prosperous, the most truly interesting to America and to humanity, more unlike and more superior to other people, (the English excepted,) than the old Roman race to their neighbors and competitors." Must this people—this national entity of New England, this "northern confederacy of superior good order," with its lofty spirit and destiny—be subject to the Virginian Jefferson and the "turbulent Parisian license of Southern Jacobinism"?[12] It is as though, ignoring the examples of John Adams and George Ticknor, Emerson harked back to the strict New England Federalists like Fisher Ames in consistently, and almost for a lifetime, virtually ruling out the possibility of any intellectual and moral interaction between New England and the South.

Yet while his attitude toward the South was as austerely inflexible as that of the most avid abolitionist, Emerson, until he became inflamed by the Fugitive Slave Act, was independent of—even hostile to—abolitionist sentiment. His attitude was governed by what may be called his "Negro problem." Although Emerson finally arrived at the conclusion that the Negro is mentally capable, he was fundamentally a white supremacist and never free from a degree of Negrophobia. The reason is clear: the mystique of the Saxon blood, always as strong in New England as in the South, was an ineradicable part of Emerson's psyche. That his was no instance of blind racial prejudice, however, is evident in the record of his long and disturbing quarrel with himself about the Negro. The drama of this is enhanced when we come to

12. *Works of Fisher Ames*, ed. W. B. Allen (2 vols.; Indianapolis, 1983), I, 216–17, 231.

it *in medias res*, for example in a journal passage in 1854, well after Emerson had been pulled into the antislavery struggle:

> The Unitarians, you say, are a poor skeptical egotistic shopping sect. The Calvinists serious, still darkened over by their Hebraistic dream. The Saxon race has never flowered into its own religion, but has been fain to borrow this old Hebraism of the dark race. The Latin races are at last come to a stand, & are declining. Merry England & saucy America striding far ahead. The dark man, the black man declines. The black man is courageous, but the white men are the children of God, said Plato. It will happen by & by, that the black man will only be destined for museums like the Dodo. Alcott compassionately thought that if necessary to bring them sooner to an end, polygamy might be introduced & these made the eunuchs, polygamy, I suppose, to increase the white births.[13]

The year before he wrote the passage just quoted, Emerson had said in his journal, under the rubric *Abolition:*

> But the secret, the esoterics of abolition—a secret, too, from the abolitionist,—is, that the negro & the negro-holder are really of one party, & that, when the apostle of freedom has gained his first point of repealing the negro laws, he will find the free negro is the type & exponent of that very animal law; standing as he does in nature below the series of thought, & in the plane of vegetable & animal existence, whose law is to prey on one another, and the strongest has it.[14]

In the same period, under the rubric *The sad side of the Negro question*, Emerson also said:

> The abolitionist wishes to abolish slavery, but because he wishes to abolish the black man. He considers that it is violence, brute force, which, counter to intellectual rule, holds property in Man; but he thinks the negro himself the very representative & exponent of that brute base force; & that it is the negro in the white man which holds slaves. He attacks . . . slaveholders north & south generally, but because they are foremost negroes of the world, & fight the negro fight. When they are extinguished, &

13. *Journals of Emerson*, XIII, 286.
14. *Ibid.*, XIII, 35.

law, intellectual law, prevails, it will then appear quickly enough that the brute instinct rallies & centres in the black man. He is created on a lower plane than the white, & eats men & kidnaps & tortures, if he can. The Negro is imitative, secondary, in short, reactionary merely in his successes, & there is no origination with him in mental & moral sphere.[15]

Such thoughts about the Negro and abolition indicate the strong persistence of the attitude toward the Negro that Emerson held long before he took a public stand against slavery. I quote from an 1840 journal entry:

> Strange history this of *abolition*. The negro must be very old & belongs, one would say, to the fossil formations. What right has he to be intruding into the late & civil daylight of this dynasty of the Caucasians & Saxons? It is plain that so inferior a race must perish shortly like the poor Indians. Sarah Clarke said, "the Indians perish because there is no place for them." That is the very fact of their inferiority. There is always place for the superior. Yet pity for these was needed, it seems, for the education of this generation in ethics. Our good world cannot learn the beauty of love in narrow circles & at home in the immense Heart, but it must be stimulated by somewhat foreign & monstrous, by the simular man of Ethiopa.[16]

Emerson eventually subscribed to the antislavery movement because it was God's way, or Nature's way, of using the hopeless plight of an inferior race in the moral education of a superior one. Yet at the same time Emerson struggled with himself about assigning the destiny of the black race to a merely expedient and subservient role in the moral economy of the universe. Perhaps after all, he decided at one point, the Negro did not belong to the fossil formations. On the contrary, "it may be that the degradation of that black race, though now lost in the starless spaces of the past, did not come without sin." If this should be so, "the condition is inevitable to the men they are, & nobody can redeem them but themselves." They must seek "an infusion from God of

15. *Ibid.*, XIII, 198.
16. *Ibid.*, VII, 393.

new thought & grace." The "exertions of the abolitionist are
nugatory except for themselves. As far as they can emancipate the North from slavery, well." In his dialectic about the
Negro Emerson wanted desperately at times to find a way of
endowing the Negro with a sense of responsibility for his
own situation, thus emancipating himself from the self-
imposed "oppression" of the emancipation movement. "Nobody can oppress me but myself," he said in accordance with
his own philosophy of individualism.[17]

In 1844, while preparing an address on the tenth anniversary of emancipation in the British West Indies at the invitation of the Concord women who belonged to the Antislavery
Society, Emerson committed to his journal a statement in
which he conferred on the "black man" the greatest potential he had discovered in man, the development of self-
reliant mind. He found his specific inspiration for this recognition in the careers of Toussaint l'Ouverture and Frederick
Douglass, though in each instance he qualified his admiration with a significant "if":

> Ideas only save races. If the black man is feeble & not important
> to the existing races, not on a par with the best race, the black
> man must serve & be sold & exterminated. But if the black man
> carries in his bosom an indispensable element of a new & coming
> civilization, for the sake of that element no wrong nor strength
> nor circumstance can hurt him, he will survive & play his part.
> So now it seems to me that the arrival of such men as Toussaint
> *if he is pure blood,* or Douglas [*sic*] *if he is pure blood,* outweighs
> all the English & American humanity. The Antislavery of the
> whole world is but dust in the balance, a poor squeamishness &
> nervousness; the might & the right is here. Here is the Anti-
> Slave. Here is Man; & if you have man, black or white is an
> insignificance.

Presumably, if either Toussaint or Douglass should be discovered to be racially impure, Emerson would have felt that
his celebration of the possibility of the black man's triumph
was invalid; if it should be found that both Toussaint and

17. *Ibid.,* VIII, 119.

Douglass show the taint of mixed blood, Emerson would have deemed jubilation to be altogether negated. Emerson affirms man to be man, regardless of color; yet he declares at the same time that man must be true white or true black to count as man. Thus holding to the color line, Emerson is prepared to say that there is now evidence that the black man has begun to help himself, and that this is reason to rejoice.

> I esteem the occasion of this jubilee to be that proud discovery that the black race can begin to contend with the white; that in the great anthem of the world which we call history, a piece of many parts & vast compass, after playing a long time a very low & subdued accompaniment they perceive the time arrived when they can strike in with force & effect & take a master's part in the music. The civilization of the world has arrived at that pitch that their moral quality is becoming indispensable, & the genius of this race is to be honoured for itself. For this they have been preserved in sandy desarts, in rice swamps, in kitchens & shoe-shops so long. Now let them emerge clothed & in their own form. I esteem this jubilee & the fifty years' movement which has preceded it to be the announcement of that fact & our anti-slavery societies, boastful as we are, only the shadow & witness to that fact. The negro has saved himself, and the white man very patronisingly says, I have saved you. If the negro is a fool all the white men in the world cannot save him though they should die.[18]

Emerson's conviction that nothing could be done for the slave save what he did for himself accounts for his failure even in his Concord "Address on the Fugitive Slave Law" seven years later (1851) overtly to join the specific issue of slavery and the problem of the nature of the American Union. He would do so only when it became a necessary strategy in the military conquest of the South by the Union forces.

Actually, Emerson's position on the character of the Union at midcentury amounted to a strategic evasion rather than a "transcendental" resolution of the slave issue. In the Slave Act speech he sought to establish the fact that "under the

18. *Ibid.*, IX, 125–26. The italics are mine.

Union" there "are really two nations, the North and the South." What severs one from the other, he argues, is not slavery but "climate and temperament." These factors account for the fact that "the South does not like the North, slavery or no slavery, and never did," although, Emerson said, the North, knowing "its own advantages," is inclined to like the South "well enough." But the alliance of the two nations must be reckoned to be at an end "as soon as the constitution ordains an immoral law," for in doing so it "ordains disunion." Anyone "who writes a crime into the statute-book digs under the foundation of the Capitol to plant there a powder-magazine, and lays a train." So with the passage of an immoral act, in this instance the Fugitive Slave Act, the preparation for the fatal explosion has been made. Americans must see to it that this law is immediately abrogated. Thereupon—and here Emerson tacitly admitted that in truth slavery was the issue in the preservation of the Union—they must support a scheme to "confine slavery to the slave states, and help them effectually make an end to it."

After plunging into a fantastic proposal for ending slavery peaceably by the purchase of the "property of the planters" with "two thousand millions of dollars" contributed through an arduous but what he deems will be an enthusiastic sacrifice on the part of the American people, Emerson speaks what for him was the truly monstrous aspect of the Fugitive Slave Act: the self-betrayal of the State of Massachusetts, which has "put itself into the base attitude of pander to the crime." This is the underlying agony in the "Address on the Fugitive Slave Law": Emerson must recognize the gross defection not only of the Union and not only of New England but in particular of his own native state from the "higher mental and moral existence" that it historically had taken the lead in establishing as the New England Way, which should properly be the American Way. Narrowing the focus of his address from the Union to Massachusetts, Emerson asks desperately: "What must we do?" and replies: "One thing is plain, we cannot answer for the Union, but we must keep Massachusetts true. It is of unspeakable importance that she play her honest part," and the honest part is for Massachusetts to recover and extend her mental and moral imperialism—the "royal position" that has been "foully lost." Observing that "Massachusetts is a little state," but that "countries have been great by ideas," Emerson points to the examples of Greece and Judea. They "furnish the mind and heart by which the rest of the world is sustained; and Massachusetts is little, but, if true to itself, can be the brain which turns about the behemoth." Emerson adds: "I say Massachusetts, but I mean Massachusetts in all the quarters of her dispersion: Massachusetts, as she is the mother of all the New England states, and as she sees her progeny scattered over the face of the land"—even, he proclaimed (a measure of his excitement, I suppose) "in the fartherest South" as well as the "uttermost West."[19]

The Emersonian drama of the self-betrayal and self-redemption of the cultural destiny of Massachusetts and New England—of the New England nation in the 1850s—reaches its climax not in the Civil War but immediately before in Emerson's reaction to "the hero of Harper's Ferry" as the embodiment of a perfect conjunction of New England spiritual nationalism, abolitionism, and Unionism. In a public speech in Boston in 1859, Emerson hailed John Brown—"the fifth in descent from Peter Brown, who came to Plymouth in the Mayflower, in 1620," and the second in descent from a captain in the Revolution—as "happily a representative of the American Republic."[20]

To understand the great attraction of Emerson to Brown, we have to remember the bitter disappointment he had experienced in certain New Englanders who had been heroes to him before the passage of the Fugitive Slave Act, particularly Daniel Webster, who as United States senator had supported

19. Ralph Waldo Emerson, *Complete Works*, ed. Edward Waldo Emerson (12 vols.; Cambridge, Mass., 1903–1904), XI, 206–12.
20. *Ibid.*, XI, 267.

the law in the name of preserving the Union, and Edward
Everett, who had defended Webster's action. In Emerson's
opinion, Webster's offense was unpardonable, being the most
egregious kind of treason, the betrayal not only of the ideals
of the American Republic, but more fundamentally of the
moral center of the Republic, and more basically still of
the moral center of New England, which reposed in the
"honor of Massachusetts." The self-proclaimed champion of
the Union had, in fact, made "the Union odious" by suc-
cumbing to the view that the protection of slavery is necessary to its preservation, whereas John Brown had glorified
the Union by declaring slavery to be its only impediment.

> He joins [Emerson told the Bostonians] that perfect Puritan faith
> which brought his fifth ancestor to Plymouth Rock, with his
> grandfather's ardor in the Revolution. He believes in two ar-
> ticles—two instruments shall I say?—the Golden Rule and the
> Declaration of Independence; and he used this expression here in
> conversation concerning them, "Better that a whole generation
> of men, women and children should pass away by a violent
> death, than that one word of either should be violated in this
> country." There is a Unionist,—there is a strict constructionist
> for you. He believes in the Union of the States, and he conceives
> that the only obstruction to the Union is Slavery, and for that
> reason, as a patriot, he works for its abolition.[21]

Although he agreed with Brown about slavery as an un-
compromisable barrier to union, Emerson at the time of
what he considered to be Brown's martyrdom was probably
not as much of a Unionist as Brown. In his "Speech on Affairs in Kansas" three years earlier, he had exalted independent statehood even if it meant not only disunion but down-
right anarchy. Brown's activities in Kansas, he said, proved
that "the terror at disunion & anarchy I hear expressed is
disappearing." With an exuberant disregard of actuality,
Emerson said that "Massachusetts, in its great day, had no
government: was an anarchy" where "every man stood on

21. *Journals of Emerson*, XI, 361, 349; Emerson, *Complete Works*, XI,
268–69.

his own feet, and was his own governor," who by exercising his independence fearlessly prevented any "breach of the peace." Even more unrealistically, Emerson called on the example of California during the gold rush days, terming this a time when every man "was armed with knife and revolver and perfect peace reigned," justice being administered instantly for "each offence." Leave slavery out of it, one might say, and Emerson in a kind of crazy way—though one must grant him poetic license—was a stronger proponent of states' rights than most southerners. He was no less so the year following the John Brown episode, when, in defending his Concord friend Frank Sanborn against the critics of his antislavery activities, Emerson warned that "as Paris has become the mistress of France, so Washington aspires to become the centre of America." The "States should resist the government," he urged, "and the cities the States, and the villages the cities."

But in his advocacy of resistance to Washington, Emerson was of course thinking of the free states; the slave states, he believed, were already perilously close to realizing the control of the nation through the centering of power in the national capital. During the Civil War Emerson thought of how it all might have been the other way around if there had been a "wiser choice of candidate by the Southern party,—say, if Jefferson Davis, instead of Pierce or Buchanan." Following the election, the southerners could have found the power to take over the army, navy, and courts, to "effect a right of transit with Slaves from state to state," and to get the "rich democrats in N Y, Pennsylvania & Connecticut to buy slaves." Then the North would have had "the like difficulty to put our states into secession as the Southerners had."[22]

In effect, at least from the time of the Fugitive Slave Law, Emerson was prepared to approve of the actual secession of the free states, or of New England, or even of Massachusetts alone, from a nation that he said in 1851 was composed at

22. *Journals of Emerson*, XV, 401.

its inception of "an intimate union between two countries, one civilized & Christian, the other barbarous, where cannibalism was still permitted." But when war came and circumstances dictated a new set of possibilities for the Washington center, he reversed his position and became an ardent Unionist. In his initial excitement indeed he advocated— thinking no doubt of the practice of the Roman Republic when the Republic was in danger—putting the Union under "the absolute powers of a dictator." Furthermore, he eagerly accepted appointment as a Visitor to West Point and found himself enthusiastic about military life as he observed it at the academy. Perhaps still more significantly, Emerson subordinated his sense of the cultural centrality of Boston and supported the desire of Charles Sumner to found a national academy of letters based in Washington in the belief that such an organization would function as the center of "very great expansion of thought & moral & practical activity" in the nation.[23] The war that had come seemed to Emerson not to be one between separate nations but a civil conflict between people of the same blood; it was a necessary process of purgation and purification of the blood of the nation.

> Let it [the War] search, let it grind, let it overturn, &, like the fire when it finds no more fuel, it burns out. The war will show, as all wars do, what wrong is intolerable, what wrong makes & breeds all this bad blood. I suppose that it shows two incompatible states of society, freedom & slavery. If a part of this country is civilized up to a clear insight of freedom, & of its necessity, and another part is not so far civilized, then I suppose that the same difficulties will continue; the war will not be extinguished; no treaties, no peace, no Constitutions can paper over the lips of that red crater.[24]

"Only when, at last," Emerson asserted, "so many parts of the country as can combine on an equal & moral contract,— not to protect each other in polygamy, or in kidnapping, or

23. *Ibid.*, XI, 354; Daniel Aaron, *The Unwritten War: American Writers and the Civil War* (Cambridge, Mass., 1973), 35n–36n. I am indebted to Aaron's singular study both generally and particularly.
24. *Journals of Emerson*, XV, 300–301.

in eating men,—but in humane & just activities,—only so many can combine firmly & durably." But Emerson said the postwar negotiation of an "equal & moral contract" with the "rebels" must be dictated wholly by the Unionists, "any & every arrangement short of forcible subjugation" being unthinkable. At the end of the war, Emerson declared that it was "far the best that the rebels had been pounded instead of negociated [*sic*] into a peace"; and he was not happy with a laxity in the terms that seemed to foreclose "any action hereafter to convict Lee of treason" and thereby prevent "the high tragic historic justice which the nation with severest consideration should execute."[25]

But for all his attraction to an integral Unionism, Emerson saw the "War of the Rebellion" through the eyes of a New England and, principally, a Massachusetts man. At the beginning of the conflict he set down in his journal a vision of the South as a "country officered from New England, preachers, teachers, editors, members of Congress, lawyers, physicians." New England, he told himself, is "a sort of Scotland"—" 'Tis hard to say why (;) climate is much: then, old accumulation of the means, books, schools, colleges, literary society. As New Bedford, is not nearer to the whales, than New London or Portland, yet they have got all the equipments for a whaler there, & they hug an oil-cask like a brother. 'Tis hard to say why: I don't know that Concord or Charles River water is more clarifying to the brain than the Savannah or Tombigbee. Yet this is your lot in the urn [world]. Cherish the school."[26] The affinity Emerson felt between Scotland and New England reflected both a certain relationship that existed for New England intellectuals between Boston and Edinburgh as cultural capitals and a marked regard for the general influence that Scottish philosophers like Dugald Stewart and Thomas Reid, critics like Francis Jeffrey and Thomas Carlyle, and periodicals like the *Edinburgh Review* and the *Quarterly Review* had had on New

25. *Ibid.*, XV, 301, 459.
26. *Ibid.*, XV, 121.

England thought. But while there was a certain parallel between the extension of the cultural influence of Scotland, as
a nation within a nation, to England and the extension of
New England's influence across America—while there was,
as Emerson suggests, a parallel between Scotland and New
England in the derivation of their authority from an undefin-
able cultural mystique—Emerson's sense of the cultural authority of New England remained primarily attached to the
mystique of a New England that had descended from the Puritan redeemers. Having saved itself from its apostasy to the
false gods of nineteenth-century materialism, New England
had at last not only conquered the barbaric South but, Emerson believed, had acquired cultural dominion over the whole
of the post–Civil War American Republic.

During the final phase of the Civil War, in October, 1864,
Emerson went to the Medford, Massachusetts, home of
George Luther Stearns, a Free-Soiler who had tried to recruit
Emerson for the antislavery movement long before he was
willing to commit himself to the cause. Here Emerson met
with Stearns, Wendell Phillips, and Joseph Smith Fowler,
state comptroller in the military government of Tennessee,
to discuss the possibilities of the future. "The conversation," Emerson noted in his journal, "political altogether, &
though no very salient points, yet useful to me as clearing
the air, & bringing to view the simplicity of the practical
problem before us. Right-minded men would very easily
bring order out of our American chaos, if working with courage, & without by-ends." He noted further that "these Tennessee slaveholders in the land of Midian are far in advance
of our New-England politicians. They see & front the real
questions. The two points would seem to be absolute Emancipation,—establishing the fact that the United States hence-
forward knows no color, no race, in its law, but legislates for
all alike,—one law for all men:—*that*, first; and, secondly,
make the confiscation of rebel property final, as you did
with the tories in the Revolution." Since the only Tennes-

sean present was Fowler, who was sympathetic to the South but opposed to slavery and presumably had no slaves, Emerson made the unlikely deduction that all the Tennessee slaveholders heartily desired a nondiscrimination mandate and the confiscation of their property. But what comes immediately thereafter in the journal record of the Medford conversation indicates that, as he had in his wholesale denunciations of the South as barbarous, Emerson easily departed from both fact and logic when the destiny of New England was involved. Through an absolute confiscation of southern property, he declared, "you at once open the whole South to the enterprise & genius of new men of all nations, & *extend New England from Canada to the Gulf, & to the Pacific.*"[27]

Emerson's seemingly boundless innocence in the face of the "practical problem" facing Americans in the aftermath of a desolating civil conflict of unprecedented ferocity was—you may judge for yourself—either abysmal or sublime. But here it was: the grandiose secular-spiritual fulfillment of Peter Bulkeley's vision of the City on the Hill—the great world-city of America, extending over the vast continental expanse, populated by superior persons from all the nations of the world, and presided over and embraced by the culture deriving from the Saxon genius of a battle-purged, purified New England. Or, more precisely, a battle-purged, purified Massachusetts.

A moment—from our perspective today—of exquisite mingling of pathos and monumental irony appears in one of his journals that Emerson entitled "War." In this we find his rough notes for a speech urging Negroes—free blacks, escaped slaves, any black available—to enlist in Robert Gould Shaw's black regiment then in the process of being formed. The reasons blacks must join up, Emerson said, is to fulfill their plain obligation to Boston. The "children of this

27. *Ibid.*, XV, 445.

famed city," Emerson proclaimed, "the children of our public schools, the children of Harvard College, the best blood
of our educated counties, object of the most romantic hope
& love, poets & romancers themselves . . . —Lander, Lowell,
Putnam, Dwight, Willard, the voice will choke to name
them"—have died because "we who resist the South, are
forced to make liberty of the negro our foundation." When
he used the word *forced,* Emerson referred to the compulsion of what he usually called the "Moral Sentiment"—
the absolute moral law, "the forces above us[,] those issues
which are made for us over our heads, paramount to our
wills." After Colonel Shaw died as he reached the top of
a parapet while spilling the blood of his black troops in
what seems to have been an unnecessary, showpiece action
against Fort Wagner in South Carolina, under siege by Federal forces, Emerson added his name to his litany of fairhaired Massachusetts heroes and wrote "Voluntaries," a
poem celebrating Shaw's obedient martyrdom to the Moral
Sentiment.

> So nigh is grandeur to our dust,
> So near is God to man,
> When Duty whispers low, *Thou must,*
> The youth replies, *I can.*[28]

In their prospectus of a more extensive inquiry into "the
mind of the planting class" than has yet been made, Eugene
Genovese and Elizabeth Fox-Genovese place a strong emphasis on the thesis Eugene Genovese has supported in *The
World the Slaveholders Made* and elsewhere: namely, that
while slavery as they knew it had a "profound racial dimension," southern proslavery advocates did not conceive of it
as a racial institution. The inner, governing logic of their advocacy of slavery centered in the case for "slavery in the
abstract"; they held that, while the racial character of its
existence had varied, slavery had been the indispensable

28. *Ibid.,* XV, 211; Emerson, *Complete Works,* IX, 207.

component of civilization.[29] Although for political reasons the advocacy of the logical implication of the case for slavery in the abstract—the extension of slavery to the southern lower-class white element—appears more by assumption than by statement, it is an idea clearly present in the thought of George Fitzhugh and other social theorists of the antebellum South.

Looking closely at Emerson's opposition to slavery—its tendency to be austerely ethical rather than humanitarian—we can hardly escape the conclusion that his inclination was to regard slavery even more abstractly than the southern apologists. But this is not surprising in view of the light of his need to accommodate slavery to his radical dictate that the "individual is the world." The stress of this accommodation intensifying with the increase of his involvement in the slavery question, by 1852 Emerson felt that he had allowed his active interest in the antislavery cause to threaten the principle that the infinite worth of the individual negates society. Declaring that in "hours of sanity, I recover myself," he admonished himself in 1852 that "God must govern his own world, & knows his way out of this pit [the slavery issue in America], without my desertion of my post which has none to guard it but me." He had, he asserted, "quite other slaves to free than those negroes, to wit, imprisoned spirits, imprisoned thoughts, far back to the brain of man,—far retired in the heaven of invention, &, which, important to the republic of Man, have no watchman, or lover, or defender, but I."

The racist indifference, if not scorn, in Emerson's reference to "those negroes"—his exclusion of the Negro from what is obviously the for-whites-only republic of man—is anticipated in a still earlier journal reflection. An entry made not long after he gave the address on "The American Scholar," it epitomizes the essential attitude, never to be

29. I refer particularly to the unpublished prospectus of their work in progress presented to the Southern Historical Association at its annual meeting, New Orleans, Louisiana, November 12, 1987.

truly altered, that Emerson assumed toward African slaves: "Lidian [Emerson] grieves aloud about the wretched negro in the horrors of the middle passage; and they are bad enough. But to such as she, these crucifixions do not come. They come to the obtuse & barbarous to whom they are not horrid but only a little worse than the old sufferings. They exchange a cannibal war for a stinking hold. They have gratifications which would be none to Lidian."[30] While the southern principle that slavery is the essential core of order and civilization was utterly anathema to his principle of individualism, Emerson had the utmost difficulty thinking of the black slave as being capable of freedom. Even as he condemned the southern slaveholders Emerson was as racist as they were, perhaps more so.

The abolition of slavery did not abolish the problem of race for Emerson. After the war, aware that problems were rising that defied the great simple answers, he became concerned about the problem of securing a broader electorate in the South by qualifying both the "mean" (or uneducated) white man and the black freedman. "We wish to raise the mean white to the right position, that he may withstand the planter," Emerson commented in his journal, but he expressed the fear that during the course of this effort the Negro might well fulfill the reading and writing requirements for voting before the "mean white" would. Emerson left the implication of his concern unstated, there being no need for him to tell himself that, while he no longer subscribed to the belief that the Negro is by nature mentally inferior to the white, the inhibitions of class and race implanted in him by the historical culture to which he belonged were too strong to be transcended. Class and race decreed that the final triumph of the imperial cultural thrust of the New England nation had been the overthrow of slavery in the abstract; the triumph would not extend to victory in concretely solving the problem presented by the existen-

30. *Journals of Emerson*, XIII, 80, V, 382.

tial condition of the freed slaves. Emerson, to be sure, did conceive of an abstract solution to the task of educating the freedman: "The way to wash the negro white is to educate him in the white man's useful & fine Arts, & his ethics."[31]

I do not suppose it is at all curious that as I set down this grand commonplace of Saxon racism, I suddenly recalled the experience of my first visit to the Boston Common and the golden-domed Massachusetts statehouse, where the long military history of Massachusetts is proudly and fiercely displayed. Leaving the statehouse, I came upon St. Gaudens' famous bronze relief depicting that doomed youth Robert Gould Shaw riding in front of a column of strangely abstract, round-cheeked, look-alike (in effect, faceless) black soldiers marching to Fort Wagner to avenge the martyred sons of Harvard, and to leave among the slain their leader, the fairest martyr of them all. Dying in obedience to the New England moral absolute, Colonel Shaw had done—in accordance with the American cult of matriarchal motherhood that first strongly manifested itself in the age of the Civil War—what every American boy must ideally do: he had fulfilled the expectation of his mother. In the "Harvard Commemoration Speech," Emerson pointed with prideful approval to all the parents of a "slaughtered son" who said, "We gave him up when he enlisted." In particular, he quoted one mother's [Mrs. Shaw's] response to the news that her son, then serving in the elite Fifth Regiment of Massachusetts, had been offered command of the Negro regiment shortly to be formed: "If he accepts it, I shall be as proud as if I had heard that he was shot."[32] Incorporated by the last great New England prophet in the sacred image of motherhood, the New England culture of mind had become an imperial culture of mind and blood.

31. *Ibid.*, XV, 459, XVI, 19.
32. Emerson, *Complete Works*, XI, 344. See also George M. Frederickson, *The Inner Civil War: Northern Intellectuals and the Crisis of the Union* (New York, 1968), 151–56.

III The South and the Lost Cause of New England

🎗

In speaking about the sacred regard that Emerson had for the New England dead of the Civil War, and of how, for all his profession of Unionism, he celebrated them as martyrs to the cause of New England, I have stressed the evidence that, in spite of his outward transformation into a Unionist, points to Emerson's unalloyed inward allegiance to the nation God had chosen the Puritans to found in New England. Emerson, it is true, had moments when he was moved by a vision of a powerful, integral American union on the way to becoming an imperialist nation-state. In 1864, when the war seemed to be entering its last phase, he declared: "The American nationality is now within the Republican Party. Hence its security. In like manner in view of all the nationalities of the world, the battle of humanity is now in the American Union, & hence the weakness of English and European opposition." Napoleon's prediction, "that, in 25 years, the United States would dictate the politics of the world," Emerson concluded, "was a little early; but the sense was just. . . . It is true, that, if we escape bravely from the present war, America will be the controlling power."[1] Yet if we compare his celebration of the increasing power of the Union and the emphasis Emerson gives to New England in his postwar comments, we realize that—although the basis of the present American nation-state was laid in the Civil War—this outcome was not his true desire. When he spoke of the Union, Emerson most often envisioned it, as he al-

1. The Journals and Miscellaneous Notebooks of Ralph Waldo Emerson, ed. William H. Gilman et al. (16 vols.; Cambridge, Mass., 1960–82), XV, 438–39.

ways had, with a New England, rather than a Washington, center, innocently considering, as I have said, that New Englanders had made a strategic alliance with the Washington power only for the sake of benefiting New England.

At Harvard's solemn commemoration of its Civil War dead on July 21, 1865, before a hushed audience of alumni and friends gathered beneath a huge tent erected on a plot adjacent to the Harvard Yard, James Russell Lowell recited a lengthy ode celebrating the Harvard scholars who had sacrificed their lives "to certify to earth a new imperial race." In his address that followed Lowell's reading, Emerson essentially provided a gloss on Lowell's image of a sacrificial certification of the culminating destiny of the chosen people of New England, their emergence as imperial conquerors. Glorifying Harvard as "parent of all the colleges," he celebrated Massachusetts as the "parent" not only of "all the North" but, through "her teachers, preachers, journalists and books" and her "religious, literary and political opinion" as the "principal planter of the Western States." The "convictions of Massachusetts" have, Emerson said, been "irresistible"; and when she had got "her blood up" she had "a fist big enough to knock down an empire."[2]

By knocking down the empire of the South, Emerson implies, New England removed the West from the threat of domination by the South and opened the vast region to the exclusive influence of its own cultural envoys. But he was strangely silent about the question of New England's postwar cultural influence on the conquered South. In fact, even though one may logically expect Emerson to have been preoccupied with the problem of reconstructing the states of the defeated Confederacy in the image of New England, he said little in this connection. Possibly his most notable comment appeared in a speech Emerson made in 1867 at the

2. James Russell Lowell, "Ode Recited at the Harvard Commemoration," in *Poetical Works of James Russell Lowell* (Boston, 1897), VIII, 28; Ralph Waldo Emerson, "Harvard Commemoration Speech," in *Complete Works*, ed. Edward Waldo Emerson (12 vols.; Cambridge, Mass., 1903–1904), XI, 343–44.

dedication of a monument to the Civil War dead of Concord. Brief, curiously retrospective, somewhat preposterous, this offers an indirect yet significant insight into Emerson's post-bellum problem with the South, particularly in one sentence he picked out to quote from a letter that a Union captain had written home after embarking on a southern campaign: "This will be a slow business, for we have to stop and civilize the people as we go along." One is inclined to wonder if this invasion strategy—blatantly snobbish and, to say the least, militarily unsound—did not have in the context of the officer's letter an ironic tone. But if so, Emerson ignored it. "The armies mustered in the North," he said, "were as much missionaries to the mind of the country as they were carriers of material force, and had the vast advantage of carrying whither they marched a higher civilization." Allowing for the fact that "there are noble men everywhere, and there are such in the South," Emerson referred to "the common people, rich or poor" of the South as "the narrowest and most conceited of mankind, as arrogant as the negroes on the Gambia River." For good measure, he said further that "it looks as if the editors of the Southern press were in all times selected from this class."[3]

Although Emerson modified his monolithic rejection of the southern character in his Concord commemoration remarks by conceding the presence of a few "noble men" in the South, he undercut his concession pretty completely by the reference to the "negroes of the Gambia River," painting with the same black brush he had picked up more than once before the war not only all southern "common people, rich or poor alike" but at least a major element of the intellectual class, the "editors of the Southern press." Earlier, I suggested that a postwar remark by Emerson expressing his concern about the possibility that the "mean white" of the South might lag behind the freed black in becoming literate revealed his continuing fear of Africanization. He projected

3. Ralph Waldo Emerson, "Dedication of the Soldiers' Monument in Concord," in *Complete Works*, XI, 355–56.

his fear more drastically when he included not only the southern literati in his perennial charge against southerners—that is, their perpetual and absolute arrogance—but likened the disposition of all "common" white southerners, "rich or poor," to that of a notably "arrogant" (or, in southern terminology, "uppity") African tribe. A somewhat more detailed illustration of how his fear of Africanization influenced Emerson will, I trust, illuminate the subject I approach at this point: namely, how the moment of the New England nation's victory over the southern nation was in truth also the moment of the defeat of New England.

Like Jefferson in the eighteenth query of *Notes on the State of Virginia*, Emerson saw slavery as the destruction of the manners of the masters. "Even the poor prisoners that starved & perished in the Libby & Andersonville prisons," Emerson reflected at the end of the war, served their cause well by "drawing out into the daylight the cruelty & malignity of the Southern people, & showing the corruption that slavery works on the community in which it exists."[4] But, more than Jefferson, Emerson was always inclined to see the "cruelty & malignity" of the masters as the result not simply of their mistreatment of the slaves in a contest of wills but of their reaction to the unredeemable African darkness in the hearts of the slaves. Even after his sympathies for the slave as a fellow human being developed and he became strongly engaged in the emancipation effort—and he would no longer, as he had once, refer to captives on a slave ship as having "exchanged a cannibal war for the stench of the hold"—Emerson continued to feel that those who dealt with slaves in the intimacy of daily encounter were subject to the influence of the jungle darkness they had carried from their African huts to their plantation cabins.

One suspects this feeling informs even one of Emerson's most bitter denunciations of the Fugitive Slave Law and Webster's role in its enactment. A satirical fantasy, to be

4. *Journals of Emerson,* XV, 458.

found in his journal for 1851, this brutal sketch—clearly based on Swift's *A Modest Proposal*—employs the boiling of babies as a metaphor for the hunting down of fugitive slaves. The satire takes off from the little-known fact that the Fugitive Slave Law of 1850 was a reenactment of a law of 1793 that had been universally ignored before the rise of abolitionism.

> In the weakness of the Union the law of 1793 was framed, and much may be said in palliation of it. It was a law affirming the existence of two states of civilization or an intimate union between two countries, one civilized & Christian & the other barbarous, where cannibalism was still permitted. It was a little gross, the task for boiling babies, but as long as this kind of cookery was confined within their [the South's] own limits, we could agree for other purposes, & wear one flag. The law affirmed a right to hunt their human prey within our territory; and this availed just thus much to affirm their own platform—to fix the fact, that, though confessedly savage, they were yet at liberty to consort with men;—though they had tails, & their incisors were a little long, yet it is settled that they shall by courtesy be called men; we all make believe they are Christians; & we promise not to look at their tails or incisors when we come into company. This was all very well. . . . But of course on their part all idea of boiling babies in our caboose was dropt; all idea of hunting in our yards fat babies to boil, was dropt; & the law became, as it should, a dead letter. It was merely there in the statute-book to soothe the dignity of the maneaters. And we Northerners had, on our part, indemnified & secured ourselves against any occasional eccentricity of appetite in our confederates by our own interpretations, & by offsetting state-law by state-laws. It was & is penal here in Massachusetts for any sheriff or town-or-state officer to lend himself or his jail to the slavehunter, & it is also settled that any slave brought here by his master, becomes free. All this was well. What Mr. Webster has now done is not only to re-enact the old law, but *to give it force,* which it never had before, or to bring down the free & Christian state of Massachusetts to the cannibal level.[5]

This bizarre vision, never lifted from his journal for publication, seems clearly to be an attempt by Emerson—how

5. *Ibid.,* XI, 354–55.

deliberate it was is conjectural—to reverse his persistent association of cannibalism with African slavery. He depicts a certain grim poetic justice: the price the white master pays for his property in his African slave is his own transformation into a cannibal. The former cannibal—now the object of Emerson's sympathy rather than his ridicule and transformed by Emerson's sympathy into a suffering human being—is eaten by his master, who in the act of possessing the African has declined into a state of barbarism far worse than that his victim had known in a natural condition of barbarism.

But the truly monstrous cost of the capture and importation of Africans into America, according to Emerson, is the price New England is paying. The citizens of "the free & Christian state of Massachusetts," if they would not break the law, have been reduced "to the cannibal level" by the traitorous act of Daniel Webster. No ordinary citizen but, in Emerson's estimation, a preeminent man of letters and a principal trustee of the moral order of society in New England, Webster had committed the unpardonable crime of defecting from the sacred order—the ideal New England order of intellectuals, or, to use the Coleridgean term (which Emerson also used at times), the New England "clerisy." For his defection, Emerson imagined that the New Englanders would surely inflict an unmerciful but just vengeance on Webster: "Tell him that he who was their pride in the woods & mountains of New England is now their mortification; that they never name him; they have taken his picture from the wall & torn it—dropped the pieces in the gutter; they have taken his book of speeches from the shelf & put it in the stove."[6]

But there were moments at the time of the Fugitive Slave Act crisis when Emerson was far less certain about New England's judgment of Webster. There was even one despairing, and revealing, moment when he found himself unable to see

6. *Ibid.,* XI, 351.

any evidence that the "sovereign superiority" of a moral and intellectual class was still exercised in New England:

> There are or always were in each country certain gentlemen to whom the honour & dignity of the community were confided, persons of elevated sentiments, relieved perhaps by fortune from the necessity of injurious application to arts of gain, and who used that leisure for the benefit of their fellow citizens in the study of elegant learning, the learning of liberty & in their forwardness on all emergences to lead with courage & magnanimity against any peril in the state. I look in vain for such a class among us. And that is the worst symptom in our affairs. There are persons of fortune enough and men of breeding & of elegant learning but they are the very leaders in vulgarity of sentiment. I need call no names. The fact stares us in the face. They are full of sneers' derision & their reading of Cicero & of Plato & of Tacitus has been drowned under grossness of feeding and the bad company they have kept. It is the want perhaps of a stern & high religious training, like the iron Calvinism which steeled their fathers seventy five years ago. But though I find the names of old patriots still resident in Boston, it is only the present venerable Mr [Josiah] Quincy who has renewed the hereditary honour of his name by scenting the tyranny in the gale. The others are all lapped in after dinner dreams and are as obsequious to Mr Webster as he is to the gentlemen of Richmond and Charleston. The want of loftiness of sentiment in the class of wealth & education in the University too is deplorable. I am sorry to say I predict too readily their feeling. They will not even understand the depth of my regret & will find their own supercilious & foppish version. But I refer them back to their Cicero & Tacitus & to their early resolutions.[7]

The only precise excuse Emerson ever devised for the treason of the man he had once inordinately admired, so far as I know at any rate, is that Webster was not a native son of Massachusetts but of New Hampshire, a state which, Emerson was sorry to say, "has always been distinguished for the servility of its eminent men." Besides Webster, Emerson in-

7. *Ibid.*, XI, 352–53.

cluded on his list of fallible New Hampshireans a good friend of Nathaniel Hawthorne, "that paltry Franklin Pierce." He could never understand what Hawthorne saw in Pierce. Yet Emerson's concern about the lack of moral fiber in the New Hampshire character was merely trivial in contrast to his apprehension about the more consequential motive for the behavior of Webster or Pierce. Placed in the context of some of his other evaluations of the intellectual and moral situation in New England, the reference Emerson makes to his fellow citizens as being as "obsequious to Mr Webster as he is to the gentlemen of Richmond and Charleston," may be taken as more than incidental. It specifically reflects the central motive of Emerson's whole lament for the decline of intellectual and moral order in New England: his conviction that New England was under the progressive influence of a "dangerous ascendency of Southern manners."[8]

As far back as 1842 Emerson had noted how "young Abolitionists" from New England who venture into Virginia "are at once hushed by the 'chivalry' which they sneer at, at home." "These southerners," he noted, "are haughty, selfish, wilful, & unscrupulous men, who will have their way, & have it. The people of New England with a thousand times more talent, more worth, more ability of every kind, are timid, prudent, calculating men who cannot fight until their blood is up, who have consciences & many other obstacles betwixt them & their wishes. The Virginian has none, & so always beats them." Emerson adds hopefully that although the Virginian "beats" the New England men of conscience "today," he loses "year by year." But ten years later, at the time of the Compromise of 1850, Emerson was complaining

that the Southerner always beats us in Politics. And for this reason, that it comes at Washington to a game of personalities. The Southerner has personality, has temperament, has manners, persuasion, address & terror. The cold Yankee has wealth, numbers,

8. *Ibid.,* XI, 345, XV, 60, XI, 349.

intellect, material power of all sorts, but has not fire or firmness, & is coaxed & talked & bantered & shamed & scared, till he votes away the dominion of his millions at home. He never comes back quite the same man he went; but has been handled, tampered with.

In this enumeration of the attributes of the southerner, which, we take it, Emerson placed in ascending order of importance, the most significant is "terror." Six years later, the word occurs again in a journal entry in connection with the South: "The literature of slave states is, the science, the morals, not encouraging. There's a kind of deviltry here. . . . The wine tastes fiery. The women have a worm between their lips. Not a gentleman, not a hero, not a poet, not a Woman, born in all that immense country! There must be such, for nature avenges herself, but they lie perdus, & make no sign in the reign of terror. In fifty years, since Mr Jefferson, not a breath of air has come to the intellect or heart."[9]

Although Emerson obviously refers to a repression of mind and spirit in the post-Jeffersonian South, he does not appear to have seen the southern "reign of terror" as resulting from the unofficial policy of censorship in the South. The terror derives from within the minds and hearts of the slaveholders, from a "deviltry" that is inescapably inherent in the possession by human beings of other human beings as property. If we go back to his 1859 list of the slaveholders' attributes—temperament, manners, persuasion, address, and terror—we may say that Emerson's ordering suggests that temperament and manners, in combination with the distinctly literary attributes of persuasion and address, produce the ultimate attribute of southerners—terror. Thus although he consistently refused to identify the South with the culture of mind, Emerson associated the southern power of terror with the personality or manners of the southern intellect—with, that is, an insidious literary power possessed

9. *Ibid.*, VII, 473–74, XI, 233, XIV, 406.

exclusively by the slaveholder. Fearing this power, he exposed the unspoken fear symbolized for him by Webster's treason: that it represented the intimidation of the New England intellect by a subtle and expanding southern literary and intellectual deviltry.

Emerson's apprehension about the possibility that he was wrong about what he had always so strenuously denied to the southern slaveholders—a literary and intellectual capacity—would seem to inform a strange passage in his most substantial reflection on the postbellum intellectual situation in America, an address to the Phi Beta Kappa Society of Harvard on July 18, 1867, entitled "Progress of Culture." Delivered thirty years after "The American Scholar," Emerson's second Phi Beta Kappa address at Harvard—in tone and content a generally optimistic summing up of an age and, indirectly, of Emerson's role in it—has a unique significance in that it may be said to be the final major pronouncement of the last of the New England prophets and lawgivers.

Arbitrarily setting aside several aspects of "Progress of Culture" that I no doubt should discuss, I shall come at once to the passage I have particularly in mind, the climactic statement, in which Emerson directly addressed not simply the youthful members of Phi Beta Kappa but the whole "assembly of educated, reflecting, successful and powerful persons" he had before him in his audience at Harvard two years after the end of the Civil War. Contemplating the mission of "scholars and idealists" "in a barbarous age" to provide calm guidance "amidst insanity" toward the goal of putting "the ideal rules" of liberty "into practice," Emerson saw courage for this task of the future in the example of the immediate past, when "the ardor of the assailant" made "the vigor of the defender."

> The great are not tender at being obscure, despised, insulted. Such only feel themselves in adverse fortune. Strong men greet war, tempest, hard times, which search till they find resistance and bottom. They wish, as Pindar said, "to tread the floors of

hell, with necessities as hard as iron." Periodicity, reaction, are laws of mind as well as of matter. Bad kings and governors help us, if only they are bad enough. In England, it was the game laws which exasperated the farmers to carry the Reform Bill. It was what we call *plantation manners* which drove peaceable forgiving New England to emancipation without phrase. In the Rebellion who were our best allies? Always the enemy. The community of scholars do not know their own power, and dishearten each other by tolerating political baseness in their members. Now nobody doubts the power of manners, or that wherever high society exists it is very well to exclude pretenders. The intruder finds himself uncomfortable, and quickly departs to his own gang.[10]

Obliquely identifying "plantation manners" as a manner of mind or thought, and thus certifying what he had said did not exist—a southern intellect—as the enemy, Emerson in effect adopted the strategy of implying that southerners were merely intellectual "pretenders" and warned against admitting such enemies of thought to the "community of scholars." Saying that "political baseness" must not be tolerated by this community, and warning against the emergence of another inside traitor like Webster, his concern was not so much simply to protect the New England mind as to preserve and protect the New England dominion against a southern mind. In the same year he gave his second Phi Beta Kappa address, I should add, Emerson confided to his journal: "No matter how hot may be the rivalry & animosity between nations, the love of the cultivated class will be to the most cultivated nation. We scold England, but we would not fight her. We loved England, but we never loved our Southern states."[11] The distinction between New England and the South would appear no longer to be simply between a civilized and a barbarous world but between a "cultivated" and a less-cultivated one.

10. Emerson, *Complete Works*, VIII, 231–32.
11. *Journals of Emerson*, XVI, 73.

This compromise renders more poignant the impression one gets in reading Emerson's journals, addresses, and essays of the Civil War and postbellum eras of a radical vision of the consequences of emancipation. Seeing emancipation as at once resulting in the progress of the culture of mind—in the transformation of all the Republic, from the Atlantic to the Pacific, from Canada to the Gulf of Mexico—into an integral part of the New England culture of mind, Emerson denied the possibility of the reconstruction of the South and accepted without regret the destruction of that substantial portion of the Republic from whence had come the author of its originating charter, the Declaration of Independence, and ten of its fifteen antebellum presidents. Obviously the emancipatory motive, if it truly ever had an idealistic cast for him, had assumed for Emerson an almost entirely ideological cast.

It is illuminating to go back to an entry in Emerson's journals written at the time of the Fugitive Slave Law, when Webster—adhering to the same line he had announced in his debate with Hayne twenty years earlier: "Liberty *and* Union, now and forever, one and inseparable!"—had made the traitorous declaration, as Emerson saw it, in his speech of March 7, 1851: "I wish to speak today, not as a Massachusetts man, nor as a northern man, but as an American. . . . I speak today for the preservation of the Union." I present the journal passage in reduced form but with the intention of retaining its essential character:

America is the idea of emancipation.

abolish kingcraft, Slavery, feudalism, blackletter [publishing] monopoly, pull down gallows, explode priestcraft, tariff, open the doors of the sea to all emigrants. Extemporize government, California, Texas, Lynch Law. All this covers selfgovernment. All proceeds on the belief that as the people have made a gov.t they can make another, that their Union & law is not in their memory but in their blood. If they unmake the law they can easily make it again. The imagination of Mr Webster thinks this Union is a vast Prince Rupert's drop which if an acre should fall out anywhere the whole would snap into a million pieces. He does not see that the people are loyal, law-abiding, have no taste for drunken soldiering or misrule or uproar but prefer order. . . .[12]

In a subsequent notation in his journal, entered apparently at the same time as the above passage, Emerson jotted down first simply "The American Idea," then followed this with the terms "emancipation," "selfreliance," "selfhelp," "advance." Right below he wrote:

> These thirty nations are equal to any work. They are to become 50 millions presently & should achieve something just & generous. Let them trample out this mischief [slavery] before it has trampled out them. For the future of slavery is not inviting. But the destinies of nations are too great for our spanning & what are the instruments no policy can show . . . ; or by what scourges God has guarded his law. But one thing is imperative, not to do unjustly, not to steal a man, or help steal him, or to call stealing honest.[13]

To understand his thought and emotion at this point in his career, we have to keep in mind that in becoming dedicated to the cause of emancipation Emerson had become more sharply aware of being a citizen of a federal union of thirty states that had been established and maintained as a slave republic. He had recognized that the Constitution of the Republic had officially sanctioned the institution of chattel slavery; that the supreme interpreters of this document had consistently upheld the right to buy, own, and sell slaves; and that, moreover, even though the slave states were constantly on edge about abolitionism, conformity to slavery (as Larry Tise suggests in his recent *Proslavery: A History of the Defense of Slavery in America, 1701–1840*) was the prime source of power and order in America. Flirting with the notion of the secession of the New England states, Emerson in the notes I have quoted from his journal in 1850 was trying to formulate a concept of power and order that could be successfully opposed to the concept that the support of

12. *Ibid.*, XI, 406.
13. *Ibid.*, XI, 407.

slavery is necessary for the maintenance of social order. The crisis of the Union in the decade of the fifties made it seem feasible to him that if Massachusetts and her satellites in New England centered on promoting emancipation as a means of order, New England could become the controlling power in the Union. When Emerson talked this kind of "secesh" language, he did not simply mouth threats, any more than a southern extremist like Edmund Ruffin uttered idle threats when he advocated secession. In a way, Emerson spoke with the authority of a certain historical precedent not available to a Ruffin, for the culture he represented held in direct memory the precedent of a secessionist movement that had reached a limited fruition one generation earlier. Emerson, in fact, had been a lad of eleven or twelve when various well-known New Englanders, including Timothy Pickering and other Massachusetts citizens, had projected an independent New England Confederation and organized the only formal secession convention held in America before the southern secession conventions.

As a historical generalization, Emerson's conception that for Americans "their Union & law is not in their memory but their blood" would seem to deny the continuing influence of the New England dissent from the Unionist principle in the Federalist period and even, for that matter, the very ideas on which the American Republic was founded. But it is pertinent to note that the Emersonian notion of a bonding by blood rather than memory may not be without intellectual credibility inasmuch as for Emerson it probably bore less relation to the concept of a nonideational primal blood bonding than to the philosophical theory that all ideas originate in sense impressions or sensations. Akin to conceptions held by the British empiricists, this was a theory that, as it was shaped in the philosophical inquiry of Count Destutt de Tracy (1754–1836), received a special name when in the first years of the nineteenth century Destutt published his *Eléments d'idéologie* (1801–1815). The term *ideology* did not

become widely employed in the nineteenth century, however, and I have not found that Emerson ever used it. It was
only after the appearance of Karl Marx's long unpublished
The German Ideology and Karl Mannheim's *Ideology and
Utopia* in the period between the world wars of the twentieth century that the term became an omnipresent one. By
then, what Destutt had referred to as a "science of ideas"
had become known as the sociology of knowledge, although
whether this is as much a poetics of knowledge as a science
of knowledge is debatable. In any event, I do not mean to say
that Emerson presents himself to us today as a sociologist
of knowledge, only to say that his journals consistently re-
veal that he was a "sociological poet," who understood, like
another sociological poet, Jefferson, how much a given modern society is an ideological fiction, shaped and governed
more by the manner than the content of its thought, yet constantly revolving around a large central idea.

Ignoring the Constitution and much of the Declaration of
Independence, but stressing by implication certain aspects
of this document, Emerson saw the idea of emancipation as
providing for a conception of the founding of the Union as an
extemporizing act. The Union is based on a Constitution
that was written down at a certain point in time, but what
was put down need not be recalled at every moment lest (as
Webster had believed) the political and social order collapse
into anarchy. "All proceeds on the belief that as the people
have made a gov.t they can make another, that their Union
& law is not in their memory but in their blood. If they unmake the law they can easily make it again." If Americans
want to emancipate themselves from a law, Emerson divined,
they can do this because they are directed by a "blood knowledge" that tells them to prefer order instead of disorder.
Since Americans have loyalty and lawfulness in their very
bloodstream, without fear of disorder they can emancipate
themselves from monarchs, priests, and hierarchical status,
from the repressions of slavery, censorship, the death pen-
alty, and tariff barriers. They can admit any and all comers to

America without fear because all people who come here are granted the "blood knowledge" of emancipation.

Why does Emerson give the appearance of having suddenly abandoned the transcendental or idealist philosophy for the empirical mode? The obvious motive of the curious journal passage defining America not as the idea (or ideal) but as the ideology of emancipation is to offer a contrast between "memory" and "idea" as sources of knowledge adapted from the sensationalist theory of knowledge, which explicitly rejects memory in favor of sensory perception as the only valid source of knowing. But the obvious motive in Emerson's meditation on memory and blood does not express his real motive. Fundamentally prompted by his sensitivity as a "sociological poet," Emerson was responding to an awareness of a subtle and elusive but disturbing extension of the range of sensory perception in his age through the development of what Nietzsche would categorize in the 1880s in *Beyond Good and Evil: Prelude to a Philosophy of the Future* as a "sixth sense."

> The *historical sense* (or the capacity for quickly guessing the order of rank of the valuations according to which a people, a society, a human being, has lived; the "divinatory instinct" for the relations of these valuations, for the relation of the authority of values to the authority of active forces)—this historical sense to which we Europeans lay claim as our specialty has come to us in the wake of that enchanting and mad *semi-barbarism* into which Europe had been plunged by the democratic mingling of classes and races: only the nineteenth century knows this sense, as its sixth sense. The past of every form and way of life, of cultures that formerly lay right next to each other or one on top of the other, now flows into us "modern souls," thanks to this mixture; our instincts now run back everywhere; we ourselves are a kind of chaos.

For Nietzsche, the irony engendered by the historical sense, a sense submissive to "plebian curiosity" about culture, defined itself in the contrast it offered to the classical sense— now disappearing in the "chaos" of democracy—of "the perfection and ultimate maturity of every culture and art, that which is really noble in a work or human being, the moment when their sea is smooth and they have found halcyon self-sufficiency, the golden and cold aspect of all things that have consummated themselves." [14]

Although a deep nostalgia for the ideal of cultural consummation as represented in the cultures of ancient Greece and Rome was expressed in the literature and art of antebellum America, the historical sensibility of the new Republic assimilated a reverence for the classical sense of cultural fulfillment to the dynamic Enlightenment ideal of the fulfillment promised by the concept of universal moral and intellectual progress, this being famously illustrated by the rapturous vision of the reality—of the truth—of history as the triumph of mind that came to the condemned French Revolutionist Condorcet in 1794. Even as he awaited execution, Condorcet expected the almost immediate historical actualization of a just and free, happy and harmonious world through the progress of thought. But as it passed into the more complex minds of Vico, Herder, Hegel, Marx, and Nietzsche, the idea of transcendent universality of purpose and direction in history, which the believers in progress had adapted from Platonic, Stoic, and Christian sources as the overall vision of history, was brought into question by an imperialistic historicism. This demanded that not only both events and people (either as individuals or societies) but ideas—and indeed mind itself—be seen as historically unique. When each national culture is held to be singular—to exhibit periods of development, consummation, and decline germane to its own history—the classical paradigm of cultural consummation, as Nietzsche observed, loses its meaning.

Paradoxically, as a modern nation develops an intense emphasis on its particularity, it tends to transform itself into an idealized version of its historical reality and thus to become an abstraction. This is so, it would seem, because of the

14. Friedrich Nietzsche, *Beyond Good and Evil: Prelude to a Philosophy of the Future*, trans. Walter Kaufmann (New York, 1966), 151–52.

effort to intensify—to ideologize—the universal values of
the classical view of culture by making them seem to be the
ideal, and the salvational, values of a particular national culture. Such an ideological process, as Emerson's ideology of
emancipation illustrates, defied any degree of ironic under-
standing on the part of those involved in it; but if the poet-
philosopher like Nietzsche distanced himself sufficiently
from the ideal and became one of the men of "historical
sense," he found in the painful, even terrifying, experience
of recognizing the ironic relativity of values—of apprehend-
ing the destruction of the ideal—the great modern subject. It
is doubtful, moreover, that in the passage into the so-called
postmodern age the poet-philosopher has found that the
subject has entirely changed.

In worrying the implications of the thesis Emerson set
forth in his journal in 1851 that "America is the idea of
emancipation," I am, as one may suppose, anticipating the
question of his survival as an idealist in the face of his own
ironic perception of American history. I would stress in this
connection that I am referring to Emerson's closeted analy-
sis of American history. The thrust of his thesis about the
idea of America as stated in the journal passage was modified in the selective public use Emerson made of it. This is
also the case with a number of passages about America in
the lifelong record of his day-to-day thinking, in which he
struggled with a discovery potentially subversive of his re-
liance on the transcendent, all-pervasive governance of the
moral law—the Moral Sentiment—that, as he said, radiates
from the center to the circumference of the universe. But it
is singularly significant that in the critical time of Webster's
defection from New England—when Emerson felt himself
compelled to commit himself to the antislavery cause—he
recorded the experience of his personal need to ground his
opposition to slavery in a radically existentialist, quasi-
sociological interpretation of the American Revolution and
the formation of the American Union; of his need to see
these events as having been the result not of the power of

mind but of the power of American blood—of, we can as-
suredly say, the only true American blood, the Saxon blood.

And yet what happened when the final crisis came? I mean
the moment when, acting on the basis of a threefold appeal to history—to the truth of the Constitution respecting
states' rights; to the truth of the biblical sanction of slavery;
to the world-historical truth of the indispensable civiliza-
tional value of slavery—the southern secessionists unmade
the Union; while at the same time the New England emanci-
pationists—with Emerson as a prominent member of the
band—reversed their attraction to secession and, in order to
emancipate the slaves, rejoined the Union. At this juncture,
if not before, Emerson must have had a clear intimation
from the "sixth sense" of an ironic discrepancy between historical actuality and his trust in the authority of the Moral
Sentiment. The meaning of his obscure struggle to confront
the intimations of the historical sense ten years earlier, one
thinks, must now surely have become plain to Emerson. But
he did not shift his ground. How could he, we must ask, have
failed to have had vivid intimations that the great civil conflict was the fulfillment of the struggle between memory
and blood he had delineated in his journal ten years before?
How could he have failed to perceive that in their progress as
the representation of the idea of emancipation Americans
had become engaged in a bloody emancipation of a second
American Republic—a modern nation-state—from the political order that, with nostalgic affection, would come to be
thought of as the "Old Republic"?

Hawthorne, Melville, and even Whitman knew what was
happening. Hawthorne most of all understood clearly that
the emancipatory motive in the Civil War had been historically implicit in the emancipation less than a century earlier
of the children of Captain John Smith from that familial seat
of empire Hawthorne recalled fondly in his final book. Published at the midpoint of the Civil War, this was a book of
essays about England entitled *Our Old Home.* Hawthorne

meant the old home of the New Englander; his unstated theme in the book is the cultural expense of the war: the New Englander's loss of identity with the Old England, in which was implicit the threatened loss of his own identity. In a letter to his English friend Henry Bright as the war loomed in 1860, Hawthorne had wondered with wry amusement whether England "if we petition her humbly enough" could "be induced to receive the New England States back again, in our old Provincial capacity." In 1863 in another letter to Bright, Hawthorne, whose attitudes toward the war had become highly suspect in some quarters, gave his ironic perception of the conflict a reverse twist: "I have been publicly accused of treasonable sympathies;—whereas I sympathize with nobody and approve of nothing; and if I have any wishes on the subject, it is that New England might be a nation by itself."[15] Hawthorne plainly foresaw with dread the loss of his homeland in the incorporation of New England into the American nation-state.

But Emerson had no share in Hawthorne's presentiment of New England's fate. During the frightening disharmony of the war years, he took his resolute stand on the abstract dictum reiterated in his Phi Beta Kappa address in 1868 on the "Progress of Culture" that a universal "mind carries the law" and history is a "slow and atomic unfolding" of mind.[16] Emerson's outlook in the crisis of the 1860s was supported by his discovery in the crisis of 1850, when, fearing the displacement of the transcendent moral law as incarnated in New England, he had projected a struggle between memory and blood that would eventuate, not in the replacement of the transcendent moral law with the Saxon blood of an Old England, but in effect in the equation of the transcendent law and the wisdom of the Saxon blood of a New England.

15. Hawthorne to Henry Bright, December 17, 1860, March 8, 1863, both quoted in Daniel Aaron, *The Unwritten War: American Writers and the Civil War* (Cambridge, Mass., 1973), 46, 48.
16. Emerson, *Complete Works*, VIII, 223.

This essentially racist vision of the New England destiny is reflected in Emerson's wartime passion for making martyrs out of the "missionaries of the mind" that New England dispatched into combat with the South. Yet in the defeat of the South in the Southern War for Independence—a civil war that was in its historical consequences a second American Revolution—New England was itself defeated. In the Emersonian dream, the truth of the New England nation would have been fulfilled in New England's becoming the embodiment of the born-again American Republic; but with the conquest of the South, New England—which in Emerson's dream would have resulted in the exclusion of the South from the new Republic, at least from meaningful participation in it—was together with the South and the West absorbed into the form that the "new" Republic actually assumed, that of the modern nation-state. The defeated nation of the South strangely became the lost cause of the New England nation.

Conceivably, the irony of the way in which the defeat of the South meant the loss of the cause of New England nationhood might have eventually forced itself into Emerson's experiential awareness had it not been for the fact that, by the time he spoke to the Harvard Phi Beta Kappa Society in 1868, he was beginning to show signs of a slow lapse into a state of senility that before his death in 1882 would render him at times unable to recognize old acquaintances. Emerson's mental lapse may be interpreted somewhat fancifully as a symbol of the psychic consequences of his persistent faith in an anachronistic New England idealism; or as an ironic visitation of historical justice upon a man who had once denied history to the extent that he had declared that he was Adam in the Garden again with "no past at his back." Or Emerson's condition may be considered as a self-willed escape from alarming intimations of history that arose, for all his dedication to the ideal, in the chaos of the postwar age from the dark dimension of the Nietzschean "sixth sense."

But none of these interpretations is firmly supported in the record of Emerson's last years. The most important record, the self-record Emerson kept day to day in his journals—not simply routinely, but compulsively, out of a lifelong psychic necessity—became mere notes as his mind dimmed. Recognizing himself that he had aphasiac tendencies, he preferred not to write, even in his journals, if he could not write well. But he continued to be a public figure and still appeared on the platform, though mostly with old lectures that bore repeating, or with lectures pieced together from passages from old ones. He also began to give performances based on the reading of selections from others, especially other poets.

According to journal notes in the 1870s, one of the poets Emerson chose to read from was—quite surprisingly—the Charleston, South Carolina, poet Henry Timrod. By popular reputation the "poet laureate of the Confederacy," Timrod served briefly in the Confederate army but soon left the ranks because of tuberculosis. Although he had doubts about secession, he turned his skill as an occasional poet to the composition of three poems that afford a classic record of the birth ("Ethnogenesis" and "The Cotton Boll," both written in 1861) and the death of the Confederacy (the 1866 "Ode Sung on the Occasion of Decorating the Graves of the Confederate Dead, at Magnolia Cemetery, at Charleston, S.C."). So far as the journal notations show, Emerson presented only the "Ode" in his public recitals, but the fact that he recommended the *Collected Poems* for purchase by the Concord Library indicates that he probably had read all of the poems.

One is curious about how Timrod's vision struck Emerson. What did he make, one wonders, of the concluding lines of "The Cotton Boll," in which the poet appeals to God for the emancipation of the South from the barbarians of the North but pledges leniency toward them when they are vanquished?

> Oh, help us, Lord! to roll the crimson flood
> Back on its course, and, while our banners wing
> Northward, strike with us! till the Goth shall cling
> To his own blasted altar-stones, and crave
> Mercy, and we shall grant it, and dictate
> The lenient future of his fate. . . .

Or one wonders what Emerson made of Timrod's expansive, idealistic vision in "Ethnogenesis" of the South as the emancipator of the world from poverty:

> For, to give labor to the poor,
>   The whole sad planet o'er.
> And save from want and crime the Humblest door,
>   Is one among the many ends for which
>   God makes us great and rich!

Or one wonders what Emerson made of the fact that the poems of the "laureate of the Confederacy" clearly suggest that the vanquished South had a high culture even in the post-Jeffersonian age—that the culture of land and slaves was also a culture of mind. One wonders most of all how Emerson felt when he read Timrod's "Ode" on the Confederate dead to New Englanders? And, too, how did he feel when he read it once to a group of American travelers in Rome, especially if any former citizens of the Confederacy had happened to be there?

> Sleep sweetly in your humble graves,
>   Sleep, martyrs of a fallen cause;
> Though yet no marble column craves
>   The pilgrim here to pause.
>
> In seeds of laurel in the earth,
>   The garlands of your fame are sown;
> And, somewhere, waiting for its birth,
>   The shaft is in the stone.[17]

In the latest biography of Emerson, Gay Wilson Allen says Emerson's attraction to Timrod is evidence of his reconcilia-

---

17. *The Collected Poems of Henry Timrod: A Variorum Edition,* ed. Edd Winfield Parks and Aileen Wells Parks (Athens, Ga., 1965), 99, 95, 128–29.

tion with the South. But, though it was becoming popular for Unionists to become reconciled to the South, Emerson hardly had the basis for reconciliation when he had never had any use for the South in the first place. I suspect something more complex was symbolized in the former New England fire-eater's public readings of Timrod. (I use the term *fire-eater* advisedly, but Hawthorne once observed that during a discussion of the war at the Saturday Club in Boston Emerson was "breathing slaughter.") Did Emerson's public acknowledgment of Timrod imply some message from the "sixth sense"—this being to the effect that he no longer recognized the spilling of blood by New England boys as having been a symbol of a sacrifice for the cause of the transcendent New England nation; that he now had had the intimation that the spilling of blood, whether on the altar of New England or the altar of the South, was a symbol of a profound, immutable historical congruity between New England and the South that could not be transcended? Possibly we can apply still more pressure to Emerson's reading of the laureate of the Confederacy as a symbolic act. When Emerson in 1850 had intuited the power of history to subject the rational mind to blood knowledge, he symbolically anticipated an ironic knowledge he would never admit to conscious reflection: that the Harvard scholars who died for New England and the Harvard scholars who died for the South had sacrificed themselves for the destruction of what they mutually believed in: the old Union, a federation of "sovereign" states, as opposed to an integral nation-state.

Although he did not initiate it and may have regarded it as simply a gesture of rapprochement, there was one act in the postbellum career of Emerson that the public interpreted as a significant event in the reconciliation of North and South. This was Emerson's journey in June, 1876, to Charlottesville, Virginia, where he fulfilled an invitation tendered by the two literary societies of the University of Virginia—the Washington Society and the Jefferson Society—to be the orator at their annual joint meeting. Accompanied by his daugh-

ter Ellen, Emerson went into the South for the first time
since as a youth he had voyaged to South Carolina and Florida. The houseguest of George Frederick Holmes, a University of Virginia professor who before the war had been one of
the most brilliant minds among the proslavery writers in the
South, Emerson was received warmly when he arrived at Mr.
Jefferson's university. But his mental and physical capacities
had failed rather distinctly by this time, and he was not
quite up to an occasion that turned out to call for an address
not before a circumspect audience that would strain to hear
every word of the low-voiced "American Sage" but before a
noisy assemblage of students, alumni, and others who were
attending the university's gala commencement-week celebration. When the "gaunt figure of the Abolitionist philosopher" passed "up the aisle" (to quote from an account in the
Richmond *Inquirer*), he was accompanied by applause, but
soon after he began to deliver an address on "The Proper
Function of the Scholar: His Relation and Duties to the
World About Him," a good many in the assemblage began to
talk audibly among themselves. In spite of a request for silence by one of the university officials, the volume of noise
rose annoyingly. Skipping several pages of his address, Emerson came to a rapid conclusion and sat down. Yet he seemed
to understand that this audience was not being deliberately
rude, that it was by its nature a mixed and restless gather-
ing that would not have been attentive to anyone. He left
Charlottesville with gratitude to his hosts.[18]

18. The most balanced and thorough account of Emerson's visit to the
University of Virginia is Hubert H. Hoeltjie, "Emerson in Virginia," *New
England Quarterly*, V (October, 1932), 753–68. Emerson's address on the
occasion will be found under the title "The Scholar" in Emerson, *Complete
Works*, X, 259–89. Gay Wilson Allen, in *Waldo Emerson: A Biography*
(New York, 1981), p. 665, gives the title of the Virginia lecture as "The Na-
tional and Permanent Functions of the Scholar." Ralph L. Rusk (ed.), *The
Letters of Ralph Waldo Emerson* (6 vols.; New York, 1939), pp. 294–95,
prints Emerson's letter of cordial thanks to George Frederick Holmes (July
2, 1876), and in a note adds a few details supplementing Hoeltjie's account.
Rusk refers to a report in the Richmond *Enquirer* of June 30, 1876, in which
Emerson's address is called "The Natural and Permanent Functions of the
Scholar."

In any event, the truth was that Emerson had come to do something more significant than make another speech. In his opening remarks, he spoke of the institution of the university and of its scholars as a part of a transcendent community of mind. An abstract statement, this had no reference to the University of Virginia or to Harvard or to any specific institution. Composed of passages idealizing the life of the scholar, which he had extracted with the help of his friend George Cabot from numerous past essays on the intellectual vocation, the whole of the Virginia address has a disembodied quality. Insofar as it has a definable tone, it is that of faintly elegiac appeal to a past idealism. But no doubt the more attentive and perceptive members of the audience in the Public Hall at the University of Virginia on June 28, 1876—among them, say, George Frederick Holmes—were shrewd enough to discern that the New England poet and scholar was there to speak by his presence more than by his words; that he had come to Charlottesville as the embodiment of an invitation to southern poets and scholars to join in a national community of scholars—in Emerson's view, the community that New England had preeminently fostered during the long night of southern barbarism. Emerson, in other words, had come to Virginia at the end of the Reconstruction era not merely to acknowledge but to bless a literary reconstruction of the South. This was the next logical step after he had accepted Timrod into the community of the idealized dead by the act of giving public readings of his "Ode" to the Confederate dead in New England—an act that by dramatic suggestion idealized the sacrifice of the fairhaired southern boys by suggesting that they had themselves become martyrs in the act of martyring Colonel Robert Shaw as he led his black soldiers in the doomed attack on Fort Wagner. Contemplating the poetry of Emerson's act of reading Timrod's "Ode" publicly, in fact, we easily envision the attack on Fort Wagner as a graphic emblem of the American community of blood and mind—a poignant symbol of the tragic symbiosis of New England and the South.

Epilogue: Why Quentin Compson Went to Harvard

Relying on the latitude allowed by the term *meditation* in the subtitle of this study, I have indulged in a discussion that has not only been speculative but at times, I fear, impressionistic. I should explain that I had originally proposed to myself to construct both a more extensive and a more tightly organized inquiry into some of the ironies of the moral and intellectual relationship between the South and New England as these may be said to center in slavery and the Civil War. I had envisioned in particular eventually getting around to the reflection of this relationship in two or three late nineteenth- and even one or two twentieth-century "poet-historians," including Mark Twain, William Dean Howells, Owen Wister, Henry James, T. S. Eliot, and that strange, recently discovered writer Arthur Inman. Before he killed himself in 1963, Inman, a native of Atlanta (who described himself as "an offspring"—"a by-product, an extension, a growth"—of the Civil War), lived in self-confinement in a darkened room in a semirespectable residence hotel in the Back Bay section of Boston, all the while devoting himself to composing a seventeen-million-word diary. Writing a review essay of Daniel Aaron's two-million-word selective edition of Inman's work, however, I realized that the broad historical and literary implications of just this one writer on my list indicated that the time and space at my disposal would be insufficient to allow inquiries into any postbellum writers.[1] But—by way of epilogue rather than formal con-

1. Lewis P. Simpson, "The Last Casualty of the Civil War," *Sewanee Review*, XCV (Winter, 1987), 149–62. See Arthur C. Inman, *The Inman Diary:*

clusion—let me refer briefly to a problem that insistently intruded itself as I tried to fathom the meaning of Arthur Inman's fate. This is the question of the fate of a fictional character, Faulkner's doomed southern youth Quentin Compson III, a Harvard student from Mississippi who tied flatirons to his feet on the night of June 2, 1910, and cast himself into the Charles River from the bridge between Cambridge and Boston (so legend has it, though Faulkner does not specify the site) known as the Anderson Bridge.

Quentin appears chiefly in two novels by Faulkner: *The Sound and the Fury* (1929) and *Absalom, Absalom!* (1936). Among the throng of people Faulkner created to inhabit the mythical county of Yoknapatawpha, Mississippi, Quentin is the only genuine persona of the author. He is also the only Faulkner character who has been remembered, as a real person might be, by a memorial plaque. Affixed to the bridge from which Quentin presumably leaped, this reads "Quentin Compson III, June 2, 1910, Drowned in the Fading of Honeysuckle." At least the plaque did read this way until it was lost during repairs to the Anderson Bridge in 1983. It was replaced with one which, for some Faulkner fans, reads less evocatively: "Quentin Compson, Drowned in the Odour of Honeysuckle, 1891–1910." The reference in either case is to Quentin's association of the story of the defeated Compsons—most notably the story of his complex involvement with his wayward sister Caddy—with the "saddest odor of all," the smell of honeysuckle in the twilight of a rainy Mississippi summer day. For twenty years, the origin of the first plaque was a secret between the two Harvard undergraduates who were responsible for making it and putting it on the bridge on June 2, 1965, the fifty-fifth anniversary of Quentin's death. In 1985, the Washington *Post* published an article revealing the names of the students: Stanley Stefanic and Tom Sugimoto, one at the time a student at the Harvard

A Public and Private Confession, ed. Daniel Aaron (2 vols.; Cambridge, Mass, 1985), II, 1563–65.

Divinity School, the other a graduate student in physics. Both were midwesterners who had gone to school in the South. This article also revealed that after the first plaque's disappearance in 1983 it was replaced by someone who is as yet unknown.[2]

But the fascinating history of the plaque is a tale in itself. I have been getting around to saying that as the feasibility of dealing with the problem of the relationship between New England and the South in terms of a panoply of writers became doubtful to me, I had the idea of holding onto Faulkner and of coming at the whole question of the New England-South relation through one question about Quentin Compson: why did he go to Harvard? With this question in mind, I even once put down the title of my project as "Why Quentin Compson Went to Harvard." But such an approach was hardly comprehensive enough to encompass an effort to suggest the large problem of relating the culture of mind in New England to the high culture of the South. Yielding to academic inhibitions, I set down the comprehensive title that is on the title page. But I could not let Quentin go. He has been present all the way along; and I think at no time more than in the problem of why Emerson found himself on the campus of the University of Virginia on a June day in 1876. The question is not only why the enfeebled and uncertain "old Abolitionist" undertook what was for him an arduous journey from his Boston-Cambridge-Concord homeland to the homeland of Jefferson, but why the Virginians invited him in the first place.

Answers to such questions belong in the context of the historical pathos of American ideality—to the history of the persistence of the idea, long after any such possibility was effectively destroyed by the Civil War, that America is an

2. Dale Russakoff, Washington *Post*, July 21, 1985, Sec. B, pp. 1, 7–8. See also "Where, Why, Whence the Plaque," *Harvard Bulletin*, June, 1972, p. 72; "Compson's Plaque's Founder Tells Its Story," *Harvard Crimson*, July 25, 1972, pp. 1, 6. I am indebted to Joseph Blotner for the last two references.

emancipation from history. When George Ticknor had come to Virginia to see Jefferson seventy years earlier, it had not troubled him that Jefferson lived in a mansion built by slave labor and not only owned but bought and sold slaves. Emerson distinctly had this problem with Jefferson. Yet ironically, one realizes, Emerson could not continue to be either an American or a New Englander after the war without reaffirming, first, the intimate connection between the Commonwealth of Massachusetts and the Commonwealth of Virginia, and, second, his personal allegiance to the author of the Declaration of Independence and founder of the University of Virginia as a prime symbol of the source of the American Republic: the ideal autonomy of mind. As for the Virginians, regardless of the fact that they had become alienated from Jefferson as a symbol of mind during the crisis of the Union, they had kept on believing in the image of mind that the author of the Declaration of Independence represented; and for this reason, in spite of their suspicion that Harvard and Yale were "abolitionist" universities that, as Jefferson once said, produced "pious young monks," they had kept on sending their sons to New England.[3] When the war was over, they could be neither Americans nor southerners without resuming the New England connection, for they were still subject to the cultural injunction that the New England institutions belonged to an older and more coherent culture of mind than theirs, and thus were both better and more prestigious representations of mind than their own educational institutions. Because he seemed to be a living embodiment of a cohesive faith on the part of southerners and New Englanders in the transcendent, emancipating power of mind, Emerson had to come back into the South before he died, and the southerners had to ask him to come.

The reason why Quentin Compson went to Harvard is re-

3. See Jefferson to Thomas Ritchie, January 21, 1816, in *Writings of Thomas Jefferson*, ed. Andrew A. Lipscomb and Albert Ellery Burgh (20 vols.; Washington, D.C., 1905), XIV, 407.

flected in an incidental but revealing way in Faulkner's response in 1959 to a young scholar who asked the by-then world-famous Mississippi author where he would like to see his manuscripts sent for permanent deposit. The reply was, "To Harvard." When asked why, Faulkner said, "They were our first university."[4] Yet, although this cultural attitude suggests a fundamental reason why thirty years or so earlier Faulkner had decided to send Quentin Compson to Cambridge, we of course have to approach the question in terms of Quentin as he is presented in *The Sound and the Fury* and *Absalom, Absalom!* For those familiar with Faulkner's life before he managed to get in the Royal Air Corps of Canada for a brief period at the end of the First World War, it is not surprising to find some aspects of the Harvard setting as depicted in *The Sound and the Fury* more reminiscent of the Yale than the Harvard campus. Faulkner had never been to Cambridge when he wrote the novel, but he had actually, though as a nonstudent, resided for a time on the Yale campus in the quarters of his close friend, Phil Stone, a student in the Yale school of law.[5] The fact that he was familiar with Yale and New Haven yet wanted Quentin to be at Harvard emphasizes the import of the remark Faulkner made years later about the placement of his manuscripts. Harvard was more poetically compatible with the drama of Quentin's unhappy destiny than Yale.

As a highly precocious young southerner—who, as Miss Rosa Coldfield tells him, would likely become a writer when he comes back from New England—Quentin appropriately goes to the primary source of the literary mind in America—to the place that was in the fading years of the American worship of ideality between the Civil War and the outbreak

4. Joseph Blotner, *Faulkner: A Biography* (2 vols.; New York, 1974), II, 1720. I am indebted also to Professor Howard R. Lamar of Yale University for allowing me to read the manuscript of his revealing essay "Yale's Southern Connections," which was presented as an Association of Yale Alumni Lecture on June 4, 1987; and as well to Cleanth Brooks, who called my attention to Professor Lamar's work and discussed his own knowledge of Faulkner's stay in New Haven.

5. *Ibid.*, I, 201–205.

of the world conflict in 1914 still the high altar of American intellectual and literary aspiration. When Quentin went to Harvard in 1910, one recalls, it was still in the "golden years" that marked the period of the final end of the old New England culture. George Santayana, who would years later write *The Last Puritan*, was still there; T. S. Eliot, an undergraduate from St. Louis—whose New England grandfather, John Greenleaf Eliot, had come to the Mississippi Valley from Harvard as a "missionary of mind"—was there writing the first version of "The Love Song of J. Alfred Prufrock." Emerson had been dead but thirty years, and the aura of the New England Renaissance still hovered about Boston, Cambridge, and Concord, as did, if more faintly, the aura of a still-older time in which the ghosts of the Revolutionary heroes mingled with the older ghosts of the Puritan founders of the New England nation.

In making Quentin's enrollment at Harvard the fulfillment not of the youth's own personal desire but that of his neurasthenic mother, Faulkner suggests all the more graphically the southern idealization of Harvard and the New England it represented, so paradoxically held in the southern mind along with a still-bitter resentment of all Yankees. It is Mrs. Compson (she calls Quentin *"my Harvard boy"*) who insists that Quentin take the money from the sale of the last forty acres of the ruined Compson plantation and go to Cambridge. And in spite of the fact that he knows he is doomed by his own desire for death, Quentin goes. His primary motive is the same one that sent the youthful Colonel Shaw to his death at Fort Wagner: he could not disappoint his mother. It is given a southern flavor in Quentin's recollection of what his father had said to him: "for you to go to Harvard has been your mother's dream for you since you were born and no Compson has ever disappointed a lady."[6]

But this reason for Quentin's going to Harvard is the mask of the real motive. Like most educated southerners, the

6. William Faulkner, *The Sound and the Fury,* ed. Noel Polk (New York, 1987), 105, 200, 204.

Mind and the American Civil War

Compsons—in spite of their resentment of New England and New England's resentment of them—are spiritual New Englanders. As he moves toward the last moment of his life, Quentin reflects elegiacally on his destiny: "I have sold Benjys pasture and I can be dead in Harvard . . . because Harvard is such a fine sound forty acres is no high price for a fine sound. A fine dead sound." The youth from a dead South did not sink himself into alien waters when he took his fatal plunge from a bridge over a river in a dying New England. The bridge over the Charles was the same bridge as the one over the Mississippi creek where he had had his encounter with Caddy's lover, Dalton Ames.[7]

Since Faulkner wrote the story of Quentin's suicide in *The Sound and the Fury* five years before he wrote the more elaborate story of Quentin's complex emotional involvement in the story of Henry Sutpen, we do not have a completely consistent character in Quentin. But Faulkner's sense of his own deep relationship with Quentin's imagination (he once compared his connection with Quentin to that of Melville with Ishmael) led him to expand the significance of Quentin in *Absalom, Absalom!* by involving him profoundly in a complex story outside that of his own family. The burden of the history of Sutpen's effort to found a dynastic family in the Mississippi wilderness becomes a part of, as Faulkner put it, the burden of "the past in the present" that has made Quentin, as he says toward the end of *Absalom, Absalom!*, "older at twenty than a lot of people who have died."[8] By this time in his short life, having assumed the burden of the history of both the aborted Sutpen dynasty and the decayed House of Compson, Quentin has in effect assumed the burden of the whole history of the destroyed world of the southern slaveholders, and in carrying his burden to the lapsed world of Emerson ineffably but poignantly added to it the burden of the literary and moral history of this world.

7. *Ibid.*, 200, 181–86.
8. William Faulkner, *Absalom, Absalom!*, ed. Noel Polk (New York, 1986), 301.

When we expose ourselves to Quentin in his full dimension—as he is both in *The Sound and the Fury* and in *Absalom, Absalom!*—we see him as emblematic of the greatest resource of Faulkner the poet-historian. He had come into a realization of the tragic and comic knowledge that Thomas Jefferson had had but refused to believe; the knowledge (summed up in Henry Timrod's "Ethnogenesis" and "The Cotton Boll") that the architects of the idealized southern slave state had had but refused to believe; the knowledge that Emerson and the other architects of the nineteenth-century ideal of the New England nation had had but refused to believe: namely, that mind, the presumed source of emancipation from history, is in its very dream of itself as the emancipator from history completely implicated—or should the term be *imprisoned!*—in the history it has not only made but, as Paul Valéry once said of the modern mind, inordinately desires to "live in."[9]

Desperately attempting to sublimate the historicism of his consciousness—the devastating self-perception, of which he is the symbol, that consciousness is history and history is consciousness—Quentin creates the dream that he is involved in an incestuous love for his sister Caddy. In this dream, he conceives that he can save Caddy from becoming a tramp, and thus from destroying the honor of their ruined family, by having them both condemned to social ostracism and finally to hell, there to be burned and purified forever by the cleansing flames. Let me quote directly from the passage in which Quentin tells his father that he, and not Dalton Ames, her actual lover, has seduced Caddy:

> and i you dont believe i am serious and he i think you are too serious to give me any cause for alarm you wouldnt have felt driven to the expedient of telling me you had committed incest otherwise and i i wasnt lying i wasnt lying and he you wanted to sublimate a piece of natural human folly into a horror and then

9. See Paul Valéry, "Freedom of the Mind," in *History and Politics*, trans. Denise Folliot and Jackson Matthews (New York, 1962), 208–209, vol. 10 of *The Collected Works of Paul Valéry*, ed. Jackson Matthews.

exorcise it with truth and i it was to isolate her out of the loud
world so that it would have to flee us of necessity and then the
sound of it would be as though it had never been and he did you
try to make her do it and i i was afraid to i was afraid she might
and then it wouldnt have done any good but if i could tell you we
did it would have been so and then the others wouldnt be so and
then the world would roar away and he and now this other you
are not lying now either but you are still blind to what is in yourself to that part of general truth the sequence of natural events
and their causes which shadows every mans brow even benjys
you are not thinking of finitude you are contemplating an apo-
theosis in which a temporary state of mind will become sym-
metrical above the flesh and aware both of itself and of the flesh
it will not quite discard you will not even be dead and i temporary and he you cannot bear to think that someday it will no
longer hurt you like this now . . .[10]

As his father recognizes, Quentin's effort to emancipate
himself from history—to redeem the pure idea of virtue and
honor by seeking absolute damnation—represents the pur-
est, most abstract ideality. Worthy in its way of the most extreme seventeenth-century Massachusetts Puritan, it is an
ideality fulfilled in a worthy descendant, a twentieth-century
Mississippi Puritan. Quentin brings his ideality to a perfect
consummation—six months before he drowns himself in
the waters of the homeland of the Mathers, Edwards, and
Emerson—when, having finished telling the history of the
house of Sutpen to Shreve McCannon, he responds to his
Canadian friend's challenge to him: "Now I want you to tell
me just one thing more. Why do you hate the South?"

"I dont hate it," Quentin said, quickly, at once, immediately;
"I dont hate it," he said. *I dont hate it* he thought, panting in the
cold air, the iron New England dark: *I dont. I dont! I dont hate
it! I dont hate it!*[11]

Quentin could not surrender the last fragment of the ideal
southern nation to history. It was better to die for the abstract ideal of southern honor on behalf of a sister who gave

10. *The Sound and the Fury*, 203.
11. *Absalom, Absalom!*, 303.

no thought to honor at all. But the spiritual New Englander who created Quentin's and Caddy's imagination of the terrors of history out of his own imagination of them could not leave Caddy (being himself, as he said, in love with her) to an unidealized damnation. In the genealogy of the Compson family he wrote fifteen years after the publication of *The Sound and the Fury*, he says of Caddy: "Doomed and knew it, accepted the doom without either seeking or fleeing it. Loved her brother despite him, loved not only him but loved in him that bitter prophet and inflexible corruptless judge of what he considered the family's honor and its doom." Accounting for the years after her affair with Dalton Ames, Faulkner says that in 1910, when she was two months pregnant with Ames's child, Caddy married "an extremely eligible young Indianian she and her mother had met while vacationing at French Lick the summer before." Divorced by her first husband, Caddy married "a minor motion picture magnate" in 1920. Divorced again in 1925, she apparently led a rootless international existence until 1940, when she "vanished in Paris with the German occupation, still beautiful and probably still wealthy too since she did not look within fifteen years of her actual fortyeight." She "was not heard of again," save, that is, that she is almost certainly the woman the "mousecolored mousesized spinster" librarian of Jefferson, Melissa Meek, saw in a picture in "a slick magazine" in the early years of the Second World War. It is "a picture filled with luxury and money and sunlight—a Cannebière backdrop of mountains and palms and cypresses and the sea, an open powerful expensive chromiumtrimmed sports car, the woman's face hatless between a rich scarf and a seal coat, ageless and beautiful, cold serene and damned; beside her a handsome lean man of middleage in the ribbons and tabs of a German staffgeneral."[12] Cotton Mather would have loved that touch.

12. "Appendix" [the Compson family] to *The Sound and the Fury* (New York, 1954), 415. The histories of the various members of the Compson family were originally written by Faulkner for *The Portable Faulkner*, ed. Malcolm Cowley (New York, 1946).

Index

Aaron, Daniel, 96
Abolitionism, 13, 31, 53–57, 82, 99
Adams, John, 3, 12–13, 32, 53
Agassiz, Louis, 2
Allen, Gay Wilson, 92
Ames, Fisher, 52–53

Bacon, Sir Francis, 11, 40
Bacon's Rebellion, 20
Barbé-Marbois, François de, 22, 26
Beverley, Robert, 19
Blacks. *See* Freedmen; Slavery
Bright, Henry, 89
Brown, John, 59–61
Buchanan, James, 61
Bulkeley, Peter, 44–45, 65
Burgh, James, 21
Byrd, William, I, 20
Byrd, William, II, 19

Cabot, George, 95
Carlyle, Thomas, 63
Carter, Landon, 19
Carter, Robert, 18, 19
Chapman, John Jay, 1–3
Chauncy, Charles, 47
Civil War: Chapman's view of, 3;
   Ticknor's view of, 9; compared
   with English civil war, 43;
   Emerson and, 62–66, 69; black
   enlistment during, 65–66, 69;
   and commemoration of dead,
   69–72; emancipatory motive in,
   88–89; defeat of New England
   in, 90
Coleridge, Samuel Taylor, 29–30
Colman, Benjamin, 47
Compromise of 1850, p. 77
Condorcet, Marquis de, 14, 86

Constitution (U.S.), 30, 46, 82
Cotton, John, 48

Davis, Jefferson, 61
Declaration of Independence, 14,
   19, 23, 29, 81, 99
Delbanco, Andrew, 42–44, 47
Descartes, René, 11
Destutt de Tracy, Count, 83–84
Dew, Thomas Roderick, 30
Diderot, Denis, 11
Douglass, Frederick, 56

Edwards, Jonathan, 45, 46–47, 48
Eliot, John Greenleaf, 101
Eliot, T. S., 96, 101
Emerson, Ralph Waldo: significance of, 1, 3, 48–49; "American
   Scholar," 2, 35, 52, 67–68, 79;
   "Historic Notes of Life and
   Letters in New England," 2; as
   Transcendentalist, 2, 49; an-
   cestors of, 44; view of slavery, 49,
   51–59, 67–68, 73–75, 87–88;
   view of South, 49–53, 58, 62, 63,
   72–73, 78–81; view of abolitionism, 53–57; individualism
   of, 56; "Address on the Fugitive
   Slave Law," 57–59; "Speech on
   Affairs in Kansas," 60–61; as
   proponent of states' rights, 61;
   view of secession, 61–62; Civil
   War and, 62–66, 69, 70; Unionism of, 62–63, 70–71; view of
   New England, 63–64, 70–71;
   view of freedmen, 68–69, 72–
   73; "Harvard Commemoration
   Speech," 69, 71; Concord commemoration remarks, 71–72;

107

of, 1–3, 13; antebellum intellectual relationship of, with South,
2–3; as truth of American Republic, 9; commitment of, to
Republic, 32; nationalism of,
35–36; secession of, 35, 82–83,
88; colonization of, 36–41; antagonism between South and, 39–
41; reaction of, to English civil
war, 42–43; covenant of, with
God, 44–48, 70, 71; Ames's view
of, 53; Emerson's view of, 63–64,
70, 76–79, 89–90; postwar cultural influence of, on South, 71–
73; southern influences on, 77–
79; relationship of, with England,
89; Civil War and, 90
New Hampshire, 77
Newton, Sir Isaac, 11, 47
Nietzsche, Friedrich Wilhelm,
85–86, 87

Ovid, 16

Paine, Thomas, 14
Parker, Theodore, 2
Parks, William, 18
Patriarchalism, 16–18
Phillips, Wendell, 64
Pickering, Timothy, 35
Pierce, Franklin, 61, 77
Pilgrims, 41
Plymouth settlement, 36, 38
Protestants, 30, 31
Puritans, 13, 42–46, 48, 70

Randolph, John, 4
Reid, Thomas, 63
Renaissance humanism, 10–11
Rousseau, Jean-Jacques, 11
Ruffin, Edmund, 83

St. Gaudens, Augustus, 69
Sanborn, Frank, 61
Sandys, George, 16
Sandys, Sir Edwin, 41
Santayana, George, 101
Scotland, 21, 63–64
Shaw, Robert Gould, 65–66, 69,
95, 101

Shelley, Mary, 24
Shepherd, Samuel, 48
Skipworth, Robert, 27
Slavery: Ticknor's view of, 9; Jefferson's views on, 13–14, 18, 22,
23–28, 73; reasons for, 20–21;
Constitution and, 30, 82; post-
Jeffersonian mind and, 30–32;
Bible and, 31; Emerson's views
on, 49, 51–59, 67–68, 73–75,
87–88
Smith, John, 36–41, 88
South: antebellum intellectual relationship of, with New England,
2–3; as truth of American Republic, 10; intellectual culture
of, 13, 14, 16–18; colonization
of, 16–18, 36, 39; men of letters
and plantation masters, 18–20;
evangelical Protestantism of, 30,
31; and post-Jeffersonian mind,
30–32; expansion of, 32; secession of, 32; antagonism between New England and, 39–41;
Emerson's view of, 49–53, 58,
62, 63, 72–73, 78–81; New
England's postwar cultural influence on, 71–73; dangerous influences of, on New England,
77–79
Stearns, George Luther, 64
Stefanic, Stanley, 97–98
Stewart, Dugald, 63
Stith, William, 18
Stoddard, Solomon, 46
Sugimoto, Tom, 97–98
Sumner, Charles, 62

Thoreau, Henry, 2
Ticknor, George, 2–7, 9–12, 14,
35, 53, 99
Timrod, Henry, 91–93, 95, 103
Tise, Larry, 82
Toussaint l'Ouverture, François-
Dominique, 56
Traditionalism, 14–15
Transcendentalism, 2, 49
Trilling, Lionel, 40
Tucker, St. George, 20
Twain, Mark, 96